CARE
OPTIONS IN
RETIREMENT

D0412466

"This book has been written to help readers through a difficult time, with the aim of navigating relatives through the complexities of the care system. It describes the services that are available to older people and it also helps relatives identify the practicalities, such as what is available, how to arrange it, how to pay for it and where to get more information."

Margaret Wallace and Philip Spiers

About the authors

Margaret Wallace qualified as an occupational therapist and has worked with older people in the NHS, social services and on a national charity helpline. She is a trustee of a local Age Concern. Margaret has had considerable personal experience of the difficulties faced by older people and their relatives when care becomes necessary.

Philip Spiers, an accountant by profession and founder of NHFA Care Advice, has been advising older people and their families on the many complex issues they need to understand when obtaining and funding care for over 17 years. Philip's expertise has been called upon by public, private and voluntary sector organisations over the years and he is regarded as one of the leading experts on the funding of care for older people in the UK.

which?
essential guides

CARE
OPTIONS IN
RETIREMENT

MARGARET WALLACE
AND PHILIP SPIERS

Which? B[ooks] [is an imprint of Which? Ltd] and published by Which? Ltd.
2 Maryleb[one] Road, London NW1 4DF
Email: boo[ks]@which.co.uk

Distributed [by Littlehampton Book Services Ltd, Faraday Close, Durrington,] Worthing,
West Sus[sex]

British Lib[rary Cataloguing in Publication Data]
A catalog[ue record for this] book is availab[le] from [the British] Library

Copyright [© Which? Ltd 2008]

ISBN 978 [1] 84490 053 4

1 3 5 7 9 10 8 6 4 2

Although the authors and publisher endeavour to make sure the information in this book is accurate and up-to-date, it is only a general guide. Before taking action on financial, legal, or medical matters you should consult a qualified professional adviser, who can consider your individual circumstances. The authors and publisher can not accordingly accept liability for any loss or damage suffered as a consequence of relying on the information contained in this guide.

All case studies are based on the authors' experience but do not describe any individual or their circumstances. The benefit rates quoted in this edition are for the financial year 2008/9. To check for any recent updates, go to www.direct.gov.uk.

Authors' acknowledgements
The authors would like to thank the following organisations for permission to publish material in this book: Elderly Accommodation Counsel (pages 15, 52–5), Laing & Buisson's 'Care of elderly people UK market report 2007' (page 164) and NHFA (page 192).

Project manager: Claudia Dyer
Edited by: Emma Callery
Designed by: Bob Vickers
Index by: Lynda Swindells
Cover photographs: Alamy (left and bottom right), iStockphoto Images (top right)
Printed and bound by VivaPress, Barcelona, Spain

Arctic Volume White is an elemental chlorine-free paper produced at Arctic Paper Hafrestroms AB in Åsensbruk, Sweden, using timber from sustainably managed forests. The mill is ISO14001 and EMAS certified, and has PEFC and FSC certified Chain of Custody.

For a full list of Which? Books, please call 01903 828557, access our website at www.which.co.uk, or write to Littlehampton Book Services. For other enquiries, call 0800 252 100.

Contents

Introduction

The good news is that we are all living longer; the bad news is that with this can often come frailty and disability and an ever increasing need for care. It is estimated that one in four adults over 65 will need some form of long-term care during their lifetime and that every year over two million people become carers.

One in five British adults has elderly parents who require care and assistance. Those of us in this position are often collectively termed the 'sandwich generation', adult children faced with the caring issues of their parents or grandparents while at the same time supporting children and grandchildren. The responsibility for decision making around caring for our older generation will, in many cases, inevitably fall on relatives and, of course, such life-changing decisions will not be easy. Needing care is not a subject most of us want to think about as we live our busy lives. So when it happens – and this can be quite suddenly, say after a period in hospital or a broken hip – we are ill-prepared to deal with the many issues and problems that face us. This is particularly the case as more and more older people own their own homes and have greater wealth than previous generations, so many will not qualify for the state funding they had, perhaps, anticipated.

For those relatives who do not live close to their family member but act as the main contact in organising care and support services, juggling the time for regular visiting and sudden crises with their own family and perhaps work commitments can lead to tensions.

❝ The 'sandwich generation' cares for parents, children and grandchildren. ❞

MYRIAD DECISIONS

For both adult children and their parents, the variety of options that may be available is bemusing to say the least, from arranging care in your relative's own home to helping him or her move into a

 In response to demand, Help the Aged, Elderly Accommodation Counsel, Counsel and Care and NHFA, Care Fees Advice have come together to launch a joined-up advisory service about housing and care options for older people, their families and carers. Called FirstStop, you can find out more on www.firststopcareadvice.org.uk.

Care options

With so many options and decisions to make, the care system can seem a daunting place. Use this page to help navigate your way through what lies ahead.

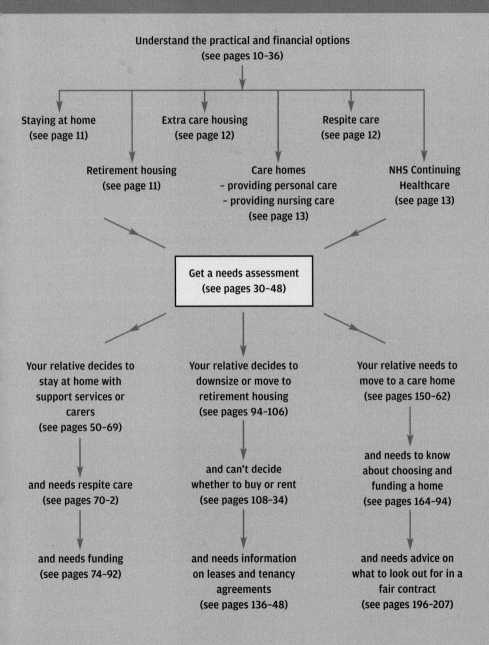

Understand the practical and financial options
(see pages 10-36)

Staying at home
(see page 11)

Extra care housing
(see page 12)

Respite care
(see page 12)

Retirement housing
(see page 11)

Care homes
- providing personal care
- providing nursing care
(see page 13)

NHS Continuing
Healthcare
(see page 13)

Get a needs assessment
(see pages 30-48)

Your relative decides to
stay at home with
support services or
carers
(see pages 50-69)

Your relative decides to
downsize or move to
retirement housing
(see pages 94-106)

Your relative needs to
move to a care home
(see pages 150-62)

and needs respite care
(see pages 70-2)

and can't decide
whether to buy or rent
(see pages 108-34)

and needs to know
about choosing and
funding a home
(see pages 164-94)

and needs funding
(see pages 74-92)

and needs information
on leases and tenancy
agreements
(see pages 136-48)

and needs advice on
what to look out for in a
fair contract
(see pages 196-207)

care home. Whatever decision is made, it can be an incredibly emotional and stressful time. On the one hand you will want the best care possible, on the other you may be feeling guilty for not providing it. And then there's the money. Who pays for what? What choice do they have? What should the state provide? Can your parents still leave the inheritance they so wished or will all their money be used for paying expensive care costs?

The important thing when dealing with this issue is to try not to panic. You need to know where to get reliable and independent information and to understand that some of the choices you and your relative will be given are not necessarily inevitable. There are often alternatives.

EASING THE BURDEN

In this book we are aiming to ease some of the burden of the decision making around choosing housing and care options for older people, including:

- Services that are available to help your relative stay at home, if that is what he or she wants to do.
- Things to think about when looking at alternative accommodation, whether this is downsizing, living with family, in a park home, retirement housing or a care home.
- If care and support are needed, no matter where, how to go about arranging it, what questions to ask and where does the state's responsibility lie in all this.

- What is available for those people who have to pay for their own care and the financial products that can potentially cap the cost.

As a relative of an older person needing care there are valuable things that you can do to give support. For example, your relative might find it quite daunting or confusing to deal with benefit claims, assessments or healthcare professionals. Understanding the labyrinth of our care system is not the easiest of tasks but one that, as a younger relative, you may find easier to manoeuvre and understand. The same goes for arranging care, managing direct payments and keeping records.

And finally, there is financial support, if you can afford it. Even though your relative might be in receipt of care services from the local council or he or she may be purchasing care privately, some supplementary support may be welcomed to make your relative's life more comfortable and enjoyable.

In this book there is a glossary and useful addresses to help you find out more details of the services described. Unless otherwise stated, all the information covers England, Wales, Scotland and Northern Ireland.

The Government has set out its long-term vision for health and social care, which has generated many headlines, but the current funding system (as featured in the book) is likely to remain for several years. *Care Options in Retirement* is therefore a source of independent information that you and your relative can rely on.

What are the options?

As people reach retirement they often start to think about making changes in their lives. Now free of work responsibilities, your relative's needs and lifestyle may change and he or she may want to consider the alternatives. Sometimes, however, illness or decreasing mobility precipitates the need for change.

Understanding the options

This chapter introduces the options that may be available to your relative. Choices range from downsizing in mainstream housing, to thinking about services or alterations that may help him or her stay at home, to moving to retirement housing, a park home, living with relatives or moving into a care home.

All these services are described in more detail in the following chapters. This chapter also describes financial benefits that may be available and how to set up a lasting power of attorney.

MEETING YOUR RELATIVE'S NEEDS

If your relative is considering changes, he or she may want to read about the different sorts of accommodation and services that are available and then try the short questionnaire on page 15.

Compromises

While your relative has choices about where and how care is provided, he or she may also have to make compromises. For example:

- If your relative cannot climb the stairs, would he or she want to live downstairs in the house, install a stair lift or move to ground-floor accommodation?
- If your relative is very frail, does he or she want to stay at home and risk being isolated – and possibly frightened – or move to extra care housing or a

> ### Jargon buster
>
> **Care package** A mixture of care and support services, often from different agencies such as social services, the housing department and the NHS to enable your relative to live at home
> **Park home** Single-storey residential mobile home
> **Telecare** Specialised form of alarm system (see page 60)

care home and risk being with people he or she may not like?
- Should care be provided at home or in a care home? While his or her lifestyle can be maintained at home, it may not be the same level of care as would be provided in a care home and your relative may get very worried if carers do not turn up as arranged.

❝ Your relative has choices but may also have to make compromises. ❞

Types of care available

This is a brief summary of the options available to your relative and of the pages where each topic is covered in detail.

Staying in your own home

Most people choose to stay at home for as long as possible. If your relative is having difficulty coping, there are now an increasing number of services that can help. These include carers, alarm systems, equipment, alterations to the home, meals at home, day centres and services to meet health-related needs. Older people who want to stay at home are often those who have (or develop) a local support network, including family, friends and neighbours.

- Information about staying at home is in chapter 3 (pages 49–72) and funding life at home in chapter 4 (pages 73–92).

Retirement housing

Retirement housing is self-contained, easily managed housing usually with some communal facilities and support on-hand if needed. It is available for people over a minimum age, usually 55 or 60, and can be rented from the council, a housing association or charity (such as an Abbeyfield House or an almshouse (see pages 101–2)), rented privately, purchased leasehold (see page 111) or as shared ownership (part rented/part bought) from a housing association.

Retirement housing appeals to people who value the safety and security it offers, are happy to pass the responsibility for maintenance and repairs of the building and upkeep of the garden to a management organisation and who like living with people of their own age. It is also a popular choice by people who are away from home for long periods and like to know that their home is safe in their absence.

- Information about retirement housing is given in chapter 5 (pages 93–106) and whether to rent or buy is covered in chapter 6 (pages 107–34).

Extra care housing

This is a form of retirement housing with personal care, meals and 24-hour support available for those that need it. Extra care housing can be rented from the council or a housing association, purchased leasehold or as shared ownership from a housing association. Extra care housing is sometimes called very sheltered housing, close care, assisted living or a retirement village. It appeals to people who like company and need the reassurance of knowing that support and help with personal care and meals is available now or in the future. It is particularly useful for couples who have different needs and it can sometimes offer an alternative to a care home.

- Information about extra care housing is in chapter 5 (pages 104–6).

Respite care

Respite care is a short period of care, usually in a care home, but sometimes at home with the help of paid carers. It is useful for people who need a short period of help, for example after an operation, to prevent a hospital admission, to give their carers a break or to see whether they like living in a care home.

- Information about respite care is in chapter 3 (pages 70–2).

"Extra care housing can be particularly useful for couples with different needs."

Care homes

A care home is a residential establishment that provides accommodation, meals and care for vulnerable older people. There are two types of care home:

- **Care homes providing personal care,** which used to be known as residential homes. These provide living accommodation, meals, help with personal care, such as dressing, supervision of medication, companionship and someone on-call at night.
- **Care homes providing nursing care,** which used to be known as nursing homes. These provide personal and nursing care 24 hours a day for people who are bedridden, very frail or have a medical condition or illness that means they need regular attention from a nurse.

A move to a care home can offer company and a safe and comfortable environment. It can also be a big relief to someone who needs a lot of care and has been struggling to cope at home, or who has become isolated and frightened or who is suffering from severe memory problems. It can also relieve the stress on relatives and carers.

- Information about care homes is in chapter 8 (pages 149–62) and paying for care homes in chapter 9 (pages 163–94).

NHS Continuing Healthcare

NHS Continuing Healthcare is for people whose primary need is for healthcare; for instance, they are in the final stages of a terminal illness, have a rapidly deteriorating condition or have care needs that are unstable, complex and unpredictable.

- For more information, see pages 182–4.

MEETING YOUR NEEDS

The role of a relative can be a difficult one. Most relatives do not live with the older person, but still act as the main contact and organiser when help and support are needed. Each person will find his or her own ways of dealing with the problems of regular visiting as well as telephoning, sudden crises and negotiating relationships with other family members, while trying to encourage the older person to continue doing as much as possible for themselves.

Tips for coping

- **If you need practical help,** such as equipment to help you lift and move your relative, or training to lift correctly, contact your relative's local council and ask for an assessment of their needs and your needs as a carer (see pages 38–46 and 47–8).
- **Look after your own health.** Talk to your GP if you are feeling very stressed, tell him or her about your caring responsibilities; your GP may be able to offer services, such as regular health checks or flu jabs.
- **If you are working,** check your legal right to request flexible working hours and to take time off to deal with an emergency. Even if you have no legal rights because of your caring duties, you may want to talk to your line

manager if, for instance, you need access to a telephone. Before doing this it is often useful to find out about your employer's policy for supporting carers, perhaps by looking in your staff handbook or talking to a welfare officer, occupational health adviser or union representative. Colleagues can also offer you support and may well be, or have been, in a similar position.

- **Involve family and friends** to make sure they know the extent of your caring duties and how they can help and support you.
- **Make sure you are getting all the financial benefits** to which you are entitled, particularly Carer's Allowance and Home Responsibilities Protection (see pages 35 and 28).
- **Talk to other people** with caring responsibilities in order to get information and support.

> **❝ Look after your own health and tell family and friends about the extent of your caring duties. Can you alter your working hours if needed? ❞**

To find your local carer's centre, contact www.carersuk.org. For Northern Ireland, ring CarersUK on 028 9043 9843. For internet users there is online support such as blogs, message boards and forums where carers can write about and share experiences. For information about legal rights and support for carers, look at: www.carersuk.org.

Getting the right help for your relative

You may want to do this questionnaire with your relative or separately and then talk about it together.

1 Is your relative finding it difficult to move around the home? Or to carry out domestic tasks, to get up and go to bed or to get help in an emergency?

If so, his or her options may be to:

- Get some domestic help or a carer.
- Use equipment such as a walking frame, bed blocks or a pick-up stick.
- Use an emergency alarm.

2 Is your relative worried about safety? Does he or she feel lonely? Does your relative use a wheelchair?

If so, his or her options may be to:

- Organise security fittings on windows and doors.
- Get an emergency alarm, a personal alarm and mobile phone.
- Investigate local facilities, clubs and specialist transport.
- Move somewhere safe and secure with company, such as retirement housing.

3 Is it difficult for your relative to live at home without support and supervision? Does he or she fall frequently?

If so, his or her options may be to:

- Install an emergency alarm or Telecare system.
- Get help in the home or a carer.
- Move to extra care housing.

4 Does your relative need a lot of help with personal care, such as using the toilet, washing and getting dressed? Is he or she unable to get a drink or meal or answer the door?

If so, his or her options may be to:

- Stay at home with a care package.
- Move to extra care housing.
- Move to a care home.

5 Does your relative have health problems that make it difficult to live at home without support? Does your relative need help to tell other people what he or she wants to do?

If so, his or her options may be to:

- Stay are home with Telecare and an intensive care package.
- Move to extra care housing.
- Move to a care home.

Planning for the future

You may well be asked to make decisions or carry out business on your elderly relative's behalf. This could be because either your relative is suffering from dementia or another disabling illness preventing him or her from being fully capable of understanding the situation, or because your relative finds it physically difficult to carry out tasks.

Decisions could be about your relative's healthcare treatment, accommodation, welfare and personal care options or financial decisions involving money and property. Nobody wants to think that at some time in the future they might be unable to make their own decisions and it's a subject that many people find difficult to broach with their parents. However, it is important and something we should all think about. Failing to prepare for the possibility of losing your mental capacity or being unable to administer your affairs effectively can lead to all sorts of complications.

There are legal mechanisms in place to protect both the decision maker and the person being cared for, which can include:

- A Lasting Power of Attorney (LPA),
- An Enduring Power of Attorney (EPA) or
- An application to the Court of Protection.

The Mental Capacity Act 2005 for England and Wales sets out who can take decisions, when and under what circumstances, and that they must be in the 'best interest' of the person who lacks capacity. The **Office of the Public Guardian (OPG)** publishes the Code of Practice to be used in assessing whether a person lacks capacity and is unable to make decisions for him- or herself at particular times. This and a copy of the Mental Capacity Act can be viewed on www.publicguardian.gov.uk.

Jargon buster

Office of the Public Guardian (OPG)
A public service that helps protect people who lack mental capacity by setting up, managing and monitoring the actions of Lasting and Enduring Powers of Attorney and appointing deputies (see page 24)

To download a copy of the Code of Practice, go to the OPG website at www.publicguardian.gov.uk.

POWER OF ATTORNEY

A power of attorney is a legal document authorising one or more persons (the attorney(s)) to act on behalf of another. An ordinary power of attorney can only be used when someone has capacity (such as if someone is abroad and needs documents to be signed in his or her absence), whereas a Lasting Power of Attorney (LPA) or an Enduring Power of Attorney (EPA) allows the chosen attorney(s) to make decisions on behalf of a person if, at a time in the future, that person lacks capacity or can no longer make decisions. The person making the power of attorney is referred to as the 'donor', and the person being given the power to act on the donor's behalf is referred to as the 'attorney'.

From 1 October 2007, as a result of the Mental Capacity Act 2005 being fully implemented, the LPA replaced the EPA, although EPAs drawn up before October 2007 can still be used.

&& There are two types of LPA, one for property and finance, the other dealing with personal welfare. ,,

LASTING POWER OF ATTORNEY (LPA)

There are two types of LPA: the Property and Affairs LPA and the Personal Welfare LPA. The two areas are treated quite separately and distinct from each other.

The Property and Affairs LPA

This form of LPA permits the attorney(s) to manage the donor's finances and property. This can be while the donor is able to make decisions but perhaps finds it difficult to do things because of a disability, illness or absence, such as collecting benefits or going to the bank. Alternatively, the LPA can be restricted for use only if, at some time in the future, the donor lacks the capacity to make such decisions for him- or herself through, say, mental illness or brain injury.

The Personal Welfare LPA

This form of LPA permits the attorney(s) to make decisions on behalf of the donor in relation to his or her health and personal welfare. This can include any decisions that are in the best interest of the donor in promoting his or her health and wellbeing, including decisions about housing, NHS treatment or care provided by social services. Unlike the Property and Affairs LPA, which can be set up to be used even if the person can still make

For more information about an EPA and the differences between an EPA and LPA, see page 22.

decisions, a Personal Welfare LPA cannot be used unless the donor lacks the capacity to make decisions about his or her welfare.

To cover both areas, the donor needs to make a separate LPA for each.

A person has to be of sound mind when drawing up an LPA, so if someone is beginning to show signs of dementia it would not be a good idea to delay taking action for too long. Both the donor and the attorney must be aged 18 or over and, in the case of the Property and Affairs LPA, the attorney cannot be bankrupt when the LPA is signed.

Restrictions

Both types of LPA can carry restrictions as to exactly what the donor wishes or does not wish to happen should decisions be made on his or her behalf. Where more than one attorney is appointed, the donor can choose whether they should act 'together' or 'together and independently'. As the phrases suggest, 'together' means all attorneys must agree to the decisions and 'together and independently' means that decisions can be made either together or by a single attorney.

The donor can instruct for different decisions to be made in different ways. For example, it might be important for two attorneys to be in agreement and administer the selling of the donor's home or making financial decisions involving large amounts of money.

Making an LPA

An LPA can be made by obtaining the Property and Affairs LPA and/or Personal Welfare LPA form from the OPG or a legal stationers (see below). Because it is such an important document and could potentially have a significant impact on the donor's future it is essential to fully discuss with all involved what exactly the document should cover. Rather than obtaining the forms and doing it yourself it may be preferential to seek professional legal advice on its completion from a solicitor who is experienced in dealing with such matters.

The LPA form is made up of three distinct parts:

- **Part A: The donor's statement.** This is where your relative enters his or her details and the details of the person(s) he or she is appointing as attorney(s). Your relative can also stipulate any guidance, restrictions or conditions on the decisions the attorney(s) can make. This part should also list the names of those to be notified (named persons) when the LPA is registered with the OPG.
- **Part B: The certificate provider's statement.** The certificate provider is someone who must speak with your relative privately to satisfy him- or herself that your relative fully understands the powers he or she

Download LPA registration packs from the OPG website at www.publicguardian.gov.uk - follow the 'Forms and booklets' tab. Or go to the legal stationers company Oyez at www.oyezformslink.co.uk.

is giving the attorney(s) and that there has been no intent of fraud or undue pressure on your relative to make the LPA. (Who can be a certificate provider is listed on the form.) Two certificate providers are required if your relative has not included any 'named persons' in part A.

- **Part C: The attorney's statement.** In part C, the attorney(s) need to provide their personal details and confirm they understand their legal duties if required to act as your relative's attorney.

Making an LPA is the only way to make plans for a time in the future when your relative may lack the capacity to make decisions for him- or herself. When choosing an attorney, it is important that the donor is confident that the attorney(s) know what he or she wants and that the donor is comfortable with the fact that those chosen will be making decisions on his or her behalf. However, there are safeguards in place to protect anyone making a LPA. These include:

- **The LPA must be registered** with the OPG before use.
- **The requirement to identify someone** to provide a Part B Certificate (see box, below left) confirming, among other things, that your relative understands the purpose of an LPA and the scope of powers he or she is giving to the attorney(s).
- **That certain persons chosen by you,** called 'named persons' (see also box, below left) are notified before registration of the LPA.
- **The signatures of the donor and attorney(s)** must be witnessed.
- **The right of specific people** (the donor, the attorney(s) and named persons) to object to registration of an LPA.
- **Attorney(s) must have regard to the Code of Practice,** which provides guidance on the Mental Capacity Act 2005. The Code makes it clear that attorneys must always act in the donor's best interests.

Optional safeguards that can also be included in the LPA are restrictions or conditions that the attorney(s) must follow. Such items could include, for example, keeping records and sharing these with someone the donor nominates, or giving guidance in the LPA, which the attorney(s) should adhere to if and when making decisions.

Guidance

The LPA form from the OPG comes with comprehensive guidance notes to enable you to fully understand each section of the form and how it should be completed. The OPG also produces booklets explaining LPAs – reference LPA102: 'A guide for people who want to make a Personal Welfare Lasting Power of Attorney' and LPA103: 'A guide for people who want to make a Property and Affairs Lasting Power of Attorney'.

Grounds for objecting to the registration of an LPA

Factual grounds

- The donor or attorney is bankrupt or an interim bankrupt, or the attorney is a Trust Corporation that has been wound up or dissolved (Property and Affairs LPA only).
- The donor or attorney is dead.
- There has been a break-up of a marriage or civil partnership between the donor and attorney.
- The attorney lacks the capacity to be an attorney or has disclaimed his or her appointment.

Prescribed grounds

- The LPA is purported not to be valid because, for example, it is considered the donor did not have capacity when making it.
- The power created by the LPA no longer exists, for example, because it was revoked by the donor when he or she had capacity.
- The donor was subjected to undue pressure and/or fraud when creating the LPA.
- The attorney proposes to contravene the powers or not behave in the best interests of the donor.

Objections should be made by completing the relevant form, which could be LPA006, LPA007 or LPA008 depending on whether the objection is from the donor, on factual grounds or is a notice of an application to make an objection. All these forms can be downloaded from the OPG website and should be accompanied by appropriate supporting evidence, which could be certification of a factual event or written and signed statements from relevant professionals.

Jargon buster

Disclaimed Decided not to accept the legal responsibility

Dissolved Closed down

Interim bankrupt Someone who is entering into an individual voluntary arrangement (IVA – a form of agreement to help recovery from debt) with his or her creditors has an interim order in place so that the creditors cannot take legal action on that person while making the IVA

Trust Corporation A legal body that provides professional legal services

Wound up Discontinued

Registering an LPA

Before you can use an LPA it must be registered with the OPG and until registration has been completed the LPA does not give the attorney(s) any legal powers to make decisions on behalf of or act for the donor. The registration can take place while the donor still has the capacity to make decisions or at any time by application from the attorney(s). Confirmation that the LPA has been registered would normally be received within five days following a six-week waiting period.

Paying for an LPA

The OPG charges a fee for registering the LPA, which would normally be paid from the funds of the donor. This fee is £150 although there are exemptions if the person liable for the fees is in receipt of the following means-tested benefits:

- Income Support.
- Income-based Jobseeker's Allowance.
- State Pension guarantee credit.

- A combination of Working Tax Credit and either Child Tax Credit, disability element or severe disability element.
- Housing Benefit or Council Tax Benefit.

Your relative will not be eligible for exemption if he or she has received a damages award of more than £16,000, which was disregarded for the purposes of determining eligibility for the benefits listed above, but he or she may be entitled to a fee remission.

If your relative does not qualify for fee exemption or remission, it is still possible to apply for it to be waived on grounds of hardship. This would need to be by writing a letter to the OPG explaining the circumstances in which paying the fee would cause hardship.

" An LPA must be registered with the OPG and there is a charge of £150 for this. "

Fee remissions for an LPA	
Income	Remission
Up to £11,500	No fee to pay
£11,501–£13,000	75% remission: your relative pays 25% of fee
£13,001–£14,500	50% remission: your relative pays 50% of fee
£14,501–£16,000	25% remission: your relative pays 75% of fee
£16,001 or more	Your relative is not entitled to a fee remission

Using an LPA

Once registered, the LPA must be presented as authorisation to whoever the attorney is dealing with in making decisions or acting on the donor's behalf. But remember that a Personal Welfare LPA can only be used once the donor lacks the capacity to make decisions.

ENDURING POWER OF ATTORNEY (EPA)

Like an LPA, an EPA (which would have been drawn up before October 2007) is different from a normal power of attorney because it continues in force even if the donor becomes mentally incapable of managing his or her affairs. An ordinary power of attorney would lapse in those circumstances, just when it was most needed. The most significant differences between an EPA and LPA are that:

- An EPA can be used without being registered until such time when the person no longer has capacity. At that time, the EPA has to be registered with the OPG (for a fee of £120) and so continues (endures). An LPA can *only* be used once it is registered.
- An EPA only enables the donor to appoint someone to manage their financial and property affairs. Unlike the LPA, an EPA cannot be made to provide the power to make decisions about the donor's personal welfare.

- An EPA does not have the built-in safeguards that the LPA has when being drawn up. However, on registration, the donor and at least three of his or her relatives must be given notice of the registration of the EPA. An objection to the registration can be made from those given notice within 35 days of the application for registration. The OPG will then consider objections to the registration on similar grounds to those for an LPA with the additional ground that the application is premature because the donor is not yet becoming mentally incapable.

While the OPG does not monitor how attorneys use their powers, once the EPA is registered and in use, if a concern that it is not being used correctly and in the best interest of the donor is reported to the OPG, they may investigate it and do have the power to see accounts or any other relevant information.

 Contact the Office of the Public Guardian (OPG) immediately if you have concerns about the actions of an attorney acting under a registered EPA or LPA, or a deputy appointed by the Court of Protection.

 For more information about the Court of Protection, go to www.publicguardian. gov.uk/about/court-of-protection.htm.

NO POWER OF ATTORNEY

If no Lasting or Enduring Power of Attorney exists and it becomes necessary to handle someone else's affairs, then to do so may mean involving the Court of Protection. The Court of Protection has the same powers as a High Court and can decide whether a person has capacity to make decisions. It exists to provide protection for people who are incapable of handling their own affairs. The Court can make declarations, decisions or orders on financial or personal welfare matters affecting the person who lacks capacity and, in doing so, must apply the principles that are set out in the Mental Capacity Act. The Court of Protection serves England and Wales and different bodies serve Scotland (the Office of the Public Guardian) and Northern Ireland (see page 25).

Applying to the Court of Protection

Applying to the Court of Protection begins with seeking 'permission' to make an application. This would not normally be required for property and affairs applications, but would be required for those relating to the personal welfare for someone who lacks capacity.

Different application forms for different circumstances are available from the Court (see below), which must be

Jargon buster

Court of Protection A court that makes decisions relating to the property and affairs as well as healthcare and personal welfare of people who lack capacity. It also has the power to make declarations about whether someone has the capacity to make a decision

accompanied by the full application fee (see box, page 24) unless exemption or remission applies.

The Court aims to deal with the permission for application within 14 days, and within 21 days of the application being made, all concerned (or persons who are likely to have an interest in the application) should be notified. If no one objects to the application during the 21 days notification period, the Court makes a decision based on the application without a Court hearing, gives directions about the application and the next steps to be taken. Alternatively, if a hearing is required, the Court fixes a date for the application to be heard by the Court.

❝ The Court of Protection is there to protect people who cannot handle their own affairs. ❞

 To find a list of forms available (there are many), go to www.publicguardian.gov.uk/forms/asking-the-court.htm. There is also a guidance booklet COP42: 'Making an application to the Court of Protection'.

The role of the deputy

The Court may appoint deputies to make decisions for people who lack capacity. A deputy is someone appointed by the Court with ongoing legal authority, as prescribed by the Court, to make decisions on behalf of a person who lacks capacity to make particular decisions, as defined by the Mental Capacity Act. The deputy would normally be someone close to your relative and he or she would need to apply to the Court by completing form COP4 stating his or her relationship or connection with your relative who lacks capacity.

Deputies must comply with the Code of Practice, which defines how the Mental Capacity Act is applied in handling someone else's affairs. They are monitored and supervised by the OPG, which might involve regular reporting, personal visits and/or other regular contact by court officials to ensure your relative's affairs are being conducted in his or her best interests. If it is considered that a deputy is not fulfilling his or her duty, the Court can discharge the deputy and seek the appointment of a new one.

Fees payable

The fee payable on making an application to start proceedings is £400. The fee is the same for making an application for permission to start proceedings for personal welfare applications.

In addition to the application fee, an appointment of a deputy incurs a fee of £125 and, for most cases, an annual Type 2 lower supervision fee of £175 is payable. However, for cases requiring Type 1 highest level supervision, the annual supervision fee would be £800. This would apply to property and affairs that are complex in nature, or if it is considered that the deputy needs supervision because there may be some doubt about his or her ability to manage your relative's affairs without it.

No supervision fees are normally payable where the value of the assets the deputy has been appointed to manage are £16,000 or less and there are no complications that would warrant a higher level of supervision.

Applying to the Department for Work and Pensions (DWP)

If your relative's income only comprises welfare benefits and a State Pension and no EPA or LPA exists, then, rather than having to apply to the Court of Protection to become a deputy, application can be made to the DWP to become an appointee so that you can receive and distribute your relative's income because he or she lacks the mental capacity to do so (see below).

 For more information about being an appointee contact the DWP. The DWP will then need to satisfy themselves that your relative is unable to manage his or her affairs and the person applying to be your relative's appointee is suitable. For the website, go to www.dwp.gov.uk.

INDEPENDENT MENTAL CAPACITY ADVOCATES

Where people who lack capacity do not have family or friends who can be involved in decision making, the Mental Capacity Act makes provision for what is called the Independent Mental Capacity Advocate (IMCA) service. This public service, details of which can be found on www.publicguardian.gov.uk, provides an independent representative who has advocacy experience in health and social care systems, IMCA training and a clear record from the Criminal Records Bureau (CRB).

IMCAs cannot act as such if they are involved in the care or treatment of the person or if they have links to the body responsible for instructing them or to anyone else involved in the person's care or treatment, other than as their advocate. Local councils and the NHS are required to appoint an advocate where decisions need to be made about serious medical treatment or moving the person to a hospital or care home. The advocate's advice must be taken into account in the decision-making process.

❝ Advocates represent people in the absence of family or friends. ❞

Northern Ireland

In Northern Ireland, the affairs of people who lack capacity are dealt with by the Office of Care and Protection details of which can be found on the website www.courtsni.gov.uk.

Northern Ireland still uses Enduring Powers of Attorney (EPA) rather than LPAs. If your relative does not have a valid EPA, then the master of the court can authorise someone to do anything that appears necessary or expedient with respect to the property and affairs of the person lacking capacity. This could be anything to do with their financial affairs including, for example, transfer and investment of money, paying bills, the sale or purchase of property, making gifts or wills or the carrying on of a business.

Such a person appointed by the master is called a 'controller' and is normally a relative or close friend although if no such person can be found to act, the master can order that the official solicitor be appointed as controller. If your relative's assets are limited and there is no real need for a controller to be appointed, the master can authorise that his or her affairs are dealt with under a Short Procedure Order, which requires your relative's means to be used sensibly and in his or her best interest.

In the case of small bank or building society account transactions or collecting benefits, application to the court may not be necessary. Most Social Security benefits can be collected by appointees.

To find out more about the IMCA service, you can download the booklet 'The Independent Mental Capacity Advocate (IMCA) service' from www.dca.gov.uk/legal-policy/mental-capacity/mibooklets/booklet06.pdf.

What benefits are available?

Many older people fail to claim all the benefits they are entitled to and collectively are missing out on millions of pounds of state support. Often it is left to relatives to understand exactly what can be claimed and make the relevant applications as attorneys or appointees. Details of the main benefits and concessions often missed are given here.

THE STATE PENSION

The State Pension is paid by the Department of Work and Pensions (DWP) when people who have fulfilled the required national insurance contribution (NIC) conditions reach pension age. This is currently 60 for women and 65 for men, although the retirement age for women will increase from 60 to 65 between 2010 and 2020.

Basic State Pension

The basic State Pension is a fixed amount payable if your relative or relative's deceased spouse or civil partner has an adequate national insurance **contribution record**, which is based on the number of **qualifying years** that contributions have been made during their working life. If your relative or relative's deceased partner does not fulfil the contribution conditions, he or she may be entitled to a reduced pension. If your relative is divorced or has a dissolved civil partnership, his or her previous partner's contribution record can be substituted for the period they were married/in civil partnership or from the beginning of your relative's partner's working life to the date the relationship was annulled.

Your relative's contribution record might well be adequate even if he or she had periods of sickness or was unemployed because he or she would have received credits in place of national insurance contributions; or, if your relative had caring or home responsibilities, his or her contribution record could have been

Basic State Pension rates

The weekly rates of basic State Pension are as follows:

- Single person £90.70
- Wife dependent on husband's contributions £54.35
- Married couple depending on husband's contributions £145.05
- Married couple/civil partners if both paid full contributions £181.40

Plus 25p if your relative is aged 80 years or over.

protected through the Home Responsibilities Protection scheme (HRP). You will be able to check on your relative's contribution record through HM Revenue and Customs www.hmrc.gov.uk.

If your relative is aged 80 or over and does not receive the basic State Pension, he or she could be entitled to a **Non-contributory Pension** of £54.35 per week. If your relative has a reduced basic pension of below £54.35 per week, because his or her national insurance contributions were inadequate, the Non-contributory Pension will bring it up to that amount.

Jargon buster

Contribution record The National Insurance contributions (NIC) paid

Non-contributory pension A pension paid to those who have not paid any or enough NIC to qualify for the full State Pension

Qualifying year A tax year in which sufficient NIC has been paid or credited to qualify for it to be counted towards a State Pension

Reduced basic pension Paid to those who have not paid sufficient NIC to qualify for a full State Pension, but have paid at least a quarter of the qualifying years needed

ADDITIONS TO THE BASIC STATE PENSION

The basic State Pension could be increased by graduated pension contributions made between 1961 and 1971 or, from 1978, through contributions made to the state-earnings related pension scheme (SERPS). Since April 2002, the State Pension can be increased by the state second pension (S2P).

The graduated pension

The size of this pension would depend on the graduated contribution made based on your relative's earnings, but normally the amount of extra pension payable is very little. Married or civil partners can inherit half of their partner's Graduated Pension as long as they were both over pension age when the partner died.

❝ Those aged 80 or over who do not receive the basic State Pension could be entitled to a Non-contributory Pension. **❞**

 For more information on the qualifying conditions for basic State Pensions, go to www.direct.gov.uk.

SERPS and S2P

Unless your relative opted out of the additional pension provisions of SERPS or S2P by taking out an occupational pension or personal pension scheme, your relative could be entitled to an additional State Pension. This would be based on contributions related to earnings and/or, in the case of S2P from April 2002, credited earnings as if your relative was earning a certain amount but unable to do so because he or she was either a low-earner, disabled or had Home Responsibilities Protection (HRP) (see box, below).

❝ Your relative could be entitled to an additional State Pension based on contributions related to earnings or credited earnings. ❞

The amount of additional pension would be based on your relative's contributions and/or credits. When a married or civil partner dies, the surviving partner can inherit some, or all, of the deceased partner's Additional Pension.

No State Pension

If your relative is not receiving a State Pension, it may be because he or she has chosen to defer it until a later date. If so, the amount received should be enhanced by an amount depending on how long it has been deferred for. Alternatively, if your relative has chosen deferment, he or she could opt for a lump sum calculated as the amount of pension that has been deferred, which has to be at least 12 consecutive months of pension, plus compounded interest for the deferred period at 2 per cent above the Bank of England base rate.

Home Responsibilities Protection (HRP)

HRP is a scheme that helps protect your basic State Pension. If you do not work or your earnings are low and you care for a child or someone who is sick or disabled, you may be able to get HRP. You are automatically entitled if you get Child Benefit in your name for a child under 16 and/or Income Support. However, if you receive Carer's Allowance (page 35), you will not be classified as needing HRP. To claim, contact your local Jobcentre Plus office and ask for the leaflet 'How to protect your State Pension if you are looking after someone at home' and claim form CF411. For further details on the eligibility criteria, visit www.thepensionservice.gov.uk.

 Full information relating to State Pensions are available from your local Pension Service office or can be found at www.thepensionservice.gov.uk. For information on deferring a pension, see the Pension Service booklet 'Your guide to state pension deferral'.

The decision to defer the State Pension will depend on your relative's circumstances. If he or she is married or in a civil partnership, deferred his or her pension and then died, your relative's spouse or partner may be entitled to extra State Pension or a lump sum. If your relative is single or widowed, his or her estate may only be able to claim up to three months of the unclaimed pension.

PENSION CREDIT

Pension Credit is a means-tested, non-taxable benefit payable in two parts: the 'guaranteed credit' and the 'savings credit'.

- **Guaranteed credit** lifts the claimant's income to the standard amounts of £124.05 per week for a single person and £189.35 for a couple.
- **Savings credit** is designed to reward people who have made some financial provision for their retirement through saving or extra income from sources, such as occupational pensions, giving them a retirement income over the amounts of £90.70 per week for a single person and £145.05 for a couple. The amount of savings credit can be up to £19.71 for singles and £26.13 a week for couples and can be paid in addition to guaranteed credit or as a stand-alone benefit. The

calculation that is used to work out savings credit is quite complicated, but as a rule of thumb it assesses how much the person's income exceeds the savings credit starting point and rewards him or her by paying an additional percentage of that amount.

To qualify for Pension Credit your relative must be aged 60 or over (65 for the savings credit), have an income below the prescribed level and be a UK resident. Applications are made as a single person or as a couple. If applying as a couple, at least one member must be of the qualifying ages.

** Savings credit rewards those who made financial provision for their retirement and can be paid in addition to guaranteed credit. **

The Pension Tracing Service

If you think your relative may have paid into a personal or occupational pension scheme but you do not have full details, you may be able to find out more through The Pension Tracing Service, which has a database of over 200,000 such schemes, and can be searched free of charge. Go to www.thepensionservice.gov.uk.

 For more information on pensions, see the *Which? Essential Guide: Pension Handbook.*

The means-test threshold

Capital is taken into account in calculating entitlement. Savings of below £6,000 per person or per couple and any deemed income from savings below this figure are ignored. Capital above this figure is assumed to produce a tariff income of £1 for every £500 or part thereof in excess of the limit. For people living in care homes, the capital threshold is higher at £10,000.

Most income is taken into account in calculating Pension Credit, but some is disregarded, including Attendance or Disability Living Allowance, Social Fund payments, charitable or voluntary payments, and the war widow's supplementary pension, which was paid to pre-1973 widows. Furthermore, some income is partially disregarded, including part of earnings or lodging income and £10 of the war widow/widower's or disablement pensions.

❝ Savings below £6,000 per person or per couple are ignored. ❞

Assessed income period

Pension Credit is awarded for an assessed income period, which is normally five years, during which time any increases in retirement income or capital are ignored by the DWP. However, if your relative's income or capital goes down during that time they can ask to be reassessed. An assessed income period ends early if your relative's circumstances change in the following ways:

● Becoming part of a couple.
● Stop being part of a couple (this could include a partner dying or moving into a care home).
● Being in hospital for more than a year.
● Moving permanently into a care home.
● Stopping receiving a pension or annuity.
● Entitlement to Pension Credit ends because he or she no longer fits the eligibility criteria.
● Your relative or his or her partner reaches the age of 65.

Additions to Pension Credit

Additions to the Pension Credit guaranteed amount can include a premium for severe disability amounting to £50.35 per person per week. To qualify, your relative must be receiving Attendance Allowance (see page 34) or the middle or higher rate of the care component of Disability Living Allowance (see page 35), be living alone and not have anyone receiving a Carer's Allowance for looking after him or her (see page 35).

It may also be possible for your relative to receive extra money if he or she has a mortgage to pay.

COUNCIL TAX BENEFIT

Council Tax Benefit (England, Wales and Scotland) is a means-tested benefit to help people on low income pay their council tax bill. It is paid directly by the local council.

To be eligible for Council Tax Benefit your relative must:

- Be living in the UK and paying council tax.
- Have savings under £16,000, unless he or she is aged 60 and over and in receipt of the guaranteed credit part of Pension Credit.

When working out your relative's entitlement to Council Tax Benefit, the local council will do the following:

- **Assess your relative and partner's (if he or she has one) combined income,** including earnings, benefits, tax credits and pension.
- **Assess your relative and partner's (if he or she has one) combined savings.**
- **Look at your relative's family circumstances,** for example, if anyone who lives in the household could help with the rent.

Check your relative is paying the right amount of council tax and is receiving any entitled discounts, such as the 25 per cent discount for a single adult living alone, or premiums, such as disability premium, severe disability premium or **second adult rebate**. If your relative has a severe mental impairment, such as Alzheimer's disease, he or she does not have to pay. If your relative is entitled to the guaranteed credit part of Pension Credit, he or she should get maximum help with council tax.

Jargon buster

Second adult rebate A form of Council Tax Benefit that can be paid if your relative shares his or her home with an adult unable to pay council tax

For more information on Council Tax Benefit, go to www.dwp.gov.uk/advisers/rr2/working/05.asp.

Applying for Council Tax Benefit and second adult rebate

If your relative is already claiming Pension Credit, he or she should automatically be given a claim form HCTB1, which covers both Council Tax Benefit and second adult rebate. Your relative needs to complete and return it to the local council offices.

If your relative's circumstances change (for example, his or her capital or income changes), he or she must tell the local council immediately.

Northern Ireland

In Northern Ireland, there is no council tax and therefore benefits are available to help pay the rates.

Rate Relief Scheme is available to pensioners on a low income and with savings of less than £50,000. Details can be found at www.lpsni.gov.uk and an online application form (form F1A 11/06) is available on www.lpsni.gov.uk/hb_rr_application.pdf.

The Lone Pensioner Allowance (LPA) was introduced on 1 April 2008. This is a non-means-tested benefit that gives a 20 per cent discount off the rates for pensioners aged 70 or over who are living on their own and paying rates for their home. For more information, contact www.helpwithratesni.gov.uk (if the home is owned) or www.nihe.gov.uk (if the home is rented).

Council tax exemption

People moving into care homes and leaving an unoccupied property should receive full exemption from council tax until it is sold.

HOUSING BENEFIT

Housing Benefit is a benefit for people living in the UK who are on a low income to help them pay their rent. If your relative lives with a partner, only one of them is entitled to Housing Benefit. To be eligible, your relative must:

- Be a tenant and responsible for paying rent to the council or a housing association.
- Have savings under £16,000, unless he or she is aged 60 or over and receiving the guaranteed credit part of Pension Credit.
- Not live in the home of a close relative.

The maximum amount of Housing Benefit that can be received is the same as the 'eligible' rent. Eligible rent includes the rent for the accommodation and charges for some services, such as lifts. Even if the rent includes water charges, charges for heating or hot water, Housing Benefit cannot cover them.

The amount of Housing Benefit that is available depends on your relative and

---

The form HCTB1 is available online at www.dwp.gov.uk/advisers/claimforms/ hctb1_print.pdf. For more information about Council Tax Benefit and second adult rebate, including advance claims, backdating and how to appeal, go to www.direct.gov.uk.

partner's (if he or she has one) personal and financial circumstances. To work out your relative's entitlement, the local council will:

- Assess your relative and partner's (if he or she has one) combined income, including earnings, benefits, tax credits and pension.
- Assess your relative and partner's (if he or she has one) combined savings.
- Look at your relative's family circumstances, for example, if the amount of rent your relative pays is reasonable for the size of his or her family and the area he or she lives in.

How to apply for Housing Benefit

In England, Wales and Scotland, Housing Benefit is paid by local councils. If your relative is already receiving Pension Credit, he or she will receive a form with those claim packs. Your relative needs to complete and return it to the local council. If your relative is not claiming other benefits, he or she can get the combined Housing Benefit and Council Tax Benefit application form (HCTB1) from the local council. Again, this form should be completed and returned to the council. This form can be downloaded from the Department of Work and Pension (DWP) website (see below).

Northern Ireland

In Northern Ireland, Housing Benefit is substantially the same as in England, Wales and Scotland. It is paid by the Northern Ireland Housing Executive and the claim form (HB1) can be downloaded from: www.nihe.gov.uk/hb1_07.pdf.

If your relative's circumstances change, for example, his or her income or savings change or your relative is going to be away from home for more than a month, he or she must tell the local council as soon as possible.

Local Housing Allowance

If your relative rents from a private landlord, a new way of calculating Housing Benefit was introduced in England, Wales, Northern Ireland and Scotland for tenancies starting on or after 7 April 2008. The application form is the same as for Housing Benefit.

Local Housing Allowance is based on the number of people in your relative's household and the local rents so may differ around the country. To check the rates in your relative's area, visit the local council website (see box below). One big difference from Housing Benefit is that the

To find your relative's local council in England or Wales, go to www.direct.gov.uk. To find a local council in Scotland, go to www.show.scot.nhs.uk. The DWP website is www.dwp.gov.uk.

Local Housing Allowance is paid directly to your relative, by cheque or into a bank account, rather than to his or her landlord.

Discretionary Housing Payments (DHP)

If your relative gets some Housing Benefit or Council Tax Benefit but the benefit does not cover all his or her rent and your relative is having difficulty in paying the shortfall, it may be possible to get DHP. DHPs are made at the discretion of the local council. Although there are no rules about who can get DHP, the local housing/council tax benefit departments usually take into account any special circumstances, such as your relative having to pay:

- Child maintenance.
- Legal costs.
- Extra heating costs if he or she is at home a lot because of sickness or disability.
- Additional travel costs, for example, to a hospital or doctor.

To apply for DHP, your relative should get a claim form from the local council.

" A local council DHP may be available to cover a shortfall in rental payments. "

INCOME SUPPORT

Income Support is a means-tested benefit from the DWP based on income and savings. It is intended to lift the recipient's income to a level where basic weekly living costs can be met. It is for people below the age of 60 years. If your relative is older, then he or she may be entitled to Pension Credit instead (see page 29).

ATTENDANCE ALLOWANCE (AA)

AA is a non-means-tested, non-taxable allowance for people aged 65 years or over who are physically or mentally disabled and need personal care to enable or help them to perform normal activities of daily living and be safe. It is also available for people who need attention or supervision by someone else. There are two rates:

- **The lower rate** (£44.85 per week) is for people who need care by day or night.
- **The higher rate** (£67 per week) is for people who need care by both day and night.

Eligibility for AA is based on the need for personal care and not on the type of disability a person might have. The person must have required the care for a period of at least six months to qualify.

For more information about Housing Benefit, including advance and backdated claims, how to appeal, pre-tenancy determinations and Housing Benefit fraud go to the Citizens Advice website: www.adviceguide.org.uk. Information about CAA and ESDA (see opposite) is to be found at www.dwp.gov.uk.

People who are terminally ill can qualify for the higher rate without having to satisfy this six-month qualifying period.

DISABILITY LIVING ALLOWANCE (DLA)

DLA is a non-means-tested, non-taxable benefit paid to people who are under 65 years, physically or mentally disabled and need help with either personal care or mobility or both. There are two components: the care component and the mobility component.

The care component

The care component is paid at three rates based on how much help with personal care your relative needs: a **lower rate** of £17.75 per week, a **middle rate** of £44.85 per week and a **higher rate** of £67 per week.

The mobility component

This is paid at two rates depending on how much difficulty your relative has walking: **a lower rate** £17.75 per week and a **higher rate** £46.75 per week.

CARER'S ALLOWANCE (CA)

CA is a non-means-tested but taxable benefit paid at the rate of £50.55 per week to people who regularly care for someone who is severely disabled, living at home and in receipt of Attendance Allowance (see opposite), or the middle or higher rate of the care component of the Disability Living Allowance. The Carer's Allowance is otherwise payable as a result of an industrial injury for people in receipt of Constant Attendance Allowance (CAA) (see below).

To qualify for CA you must be aged 16 or over and spend at least 35 hours a week caring for the person. The benefit is reduced by the amount of certain other benefits you receive, including State Pension. Therefore, CA will not be paid if you receive other benefits of £50.55 or more a week. Payment of CA is taken into account in full in the calculation of income-related benefits and Pension Credit. For Pension Credit, the amount used to work out how much you are entitled to is increased (see page 29).

CAA and ESDA (Exceptionally Severe Disablement Allowance)

To be eligible for Constant Attendance Allowance (CAA), your relative must be claiming Industrial Injuries Disablement Benefit, be 100 per cent disabled and need daily care and attention; or be claiming War Disablement Pension, be receiving a war pension of at least 80 per cent and need personal help for the same reason as they get the war pension. The CAA is paid at four different rates, ranging from £27.40 to £109.60 per week, depending on the extent of your relative's disability and the amount of care he or she needs. Exceptionally Severe Disablement Allowance is an extra allowance that could be paid at the rate of £54.80 per week if your relative is exceptionally severely disabled, already entitled to CAA and his or her need for care and attention is considered to be permanent.

Additions to Carer's Allowance

If you receive CA or have entitlement to it, you will qualify for the Carer Premium of £27.75 per week in Income Support and Income-based Jobseeker's Allowance. The Carer Premium is taken into account in calculations for Housing Benefit (see page 32) or Council Tax Benefit (see page 31). An additional amount may also be paid for your spouse or civil partner or someone living with you and looking after your dependent children. However, if you receive Child Tax Credit, any CA received will be taken into account as income.

WINTER FUEL PAYMENT

Winter Fuel Payment is an annual amount paid to people aged 60 years or over in the week commencing with the third Monday in September in the year of claim. It is paid by the Social Fund through the Department of Work and Pensions (DWP). The amount paid depends on individual circumstances:

- If your relative lives alone or is the only person in the household who qualifies for a Winter Fuel Payment or gets Pension Credit, £200 is paid if they are aged 60–79 or £300 if aged 80 or over.

- If your relative lives with at least one other person who qualifies and does not get Pension Credit, the amount paid is £100 for each qualifying person in the household aged 60–79 and £150 each if at least two people are aged 80 or over. If your relative is the only person aged 80 or over, he or she gets £200, while those below 80 in the same household continue to receive £100.

People living in care homes aged 60–79 and not in receipt of Pension Credit are entitled to £100. People aged 80 years or over are entitled to £150.

Applying for Winter Fuel Payment

Your relative would only need to make a claim if he or she was not receiving any state benefits, in which case, he or she should contact the Pension Service Winter Fuel Payment helpline on 08459 15 15 15 (08545 601 5613 for text phone users), or by getting a claim form WFP1(R) from the Pension Service website: www.thepensionservice.gov.uk/winterfuel.

All claims must reach the Winter Fuel Payment Centre by the 30 March following the winter that is being claimed for.

For more information about the CA and Carer Premium and how to apply for them, go to www.direct.gov.uk.

Getting an assessment

An assessment is the all-important first stage in getting help and support for your relative. This chapter describes the assessment process and includes topics such as whether your relative is eligible for a needs assessment, how to go about organising it, how to help your relative prepare for the assessment and the local council's eligibility criteria.

The needs assessment

The local council must assess your relative's needs before providing or arranging any services for them. It is essential to have an assessment if your relative is likely to need financial help from the council. If he or she is paying for care, it is still a good idea to have an assessment because that will help you and your relative decide what sort of care is needed.

IS YOUR RELATIVE ELIGIBLE FOR AN ASSESSMENT?

Local councils must assess anyone who appears to be in need of a community care service that is provided by the council. Community care services include:

- Home care.
- Meals on wheels.
- Day care.
- Equipment and alterations to your relative's home.
- Care in a care home.
- Respite care.

Local councils must also assess anyone who has a disability. There is no charge for an assessment.

There are no national eligibility criteria for community care services, so each council sets its own criteria, which must be based on government guidance. Each council also produces a long-term charter called 'Better care, higher standards', which describes how the assessment process works in their local area. This is available from the local council offices, library, GP's surgery and the local Age Concern. It is usually also available on the council's website.

The three stages of an assessment

There are three stages of the assessment process:

Stage 1 The assessment of your relative's needs.

Stage 2 The council decides whether it will provide or arrange services for your relative. It makes this decision by comparing your relative's assessed needs with the eligibility criteria it has set for community care services.

Stage 3 A means test. The council should only consider your relative's finances once they have agreed to provide or arrange the necessary services.

Details of the means test for people who are living at home are covered in chapter 4 (see pages 74–8) and the means tests for people who are moving into a care home are covered in chapter 9 (see page 166).

GETTING AN ASSESSMENT

To get an assessment, your relative should contact his or her local council social services department (sometimes called adult services or customer service duty team, social work department in Scotland or health and social services boards in Northern Ireland) by phone or letter and ask for a needs assessment (it is also sometimes called a care assessment). Alternatively, a relative, friend, GP, community nurse or other professional worker can contact the council on your relative's behalf, providing they have your relative's permission.

Most assessments will be carried out by a social worker or care manager from the social services department to decide whether your relative is able to live safely and independently at home. It is a good idea for you or another family member or friend to be present at the assessment.

Timescale

There are no national rules that set out how quickly a local council must carry out the needs assessment. The length of time your relative has to wait will depend on the urgency of his or her need and how much your relative is at risk because of his or her problems. Many councils set their own targets for the time by which an assessment should start. These targets are usually published in the local 'Better care, higher standards' charter.

If the local council fails to meet the targets it has set or to carry out an assessment within a reasonable time, you or your relative can make a formal complaint. For information about complaints see page 203.

> **❝ It is always a good idea for you or another family member to be present at a needs assessment. ❞**

THE ASSESSMENT PROCESS

Government guidelines state that assessments should be carried out under the Single Assessment Process (SAP) in England, the Unified Assessment (UA) in Wales and the Single Shared Assessment (SSA) process in Scotland. This means that in whichever country your relative lives, he or she will only have one assessment covering both health and social services, although the assessment may be spread over several visits to your relative's home.

The SAP, UA and SSA was set up so that staff from different agencies could work together to ensure that your relative receives the best possible care and does not have duplicate assessments from different people.

To find your relative's local council in England or Wales, go to www.direct.gov.uk.
To find a local council in Scotland, go to www.show.scot.nhs.uk.

The type of assessment your relative has will depend on his or her needs (see the box, below).

"The four types of care assessment range from considering specialist equipment to a detailed overview. "

Northern Ireland

In Northern Ireland, your relative's local Health and Social Services Board will explain the assessment process in their area, which varies from place to place. To find information about devolved services in Northern Ireland, look at www.direct.gov.uk. To find information about Health and Social Services Boards look at www.onlineni.net.

Different types of assessment

In England and Wales, the Single Assessment Process and Unified Assessment Process sets out four types of assessment:

- A **contact assessment** is often the first contact between the older person and the local council and is the point at which basic personal information is gathered and it also identifies if a further assessment is needed. Sometimes this may be carried out over the telephone or your relative may complete a form. If there are further needs/risks, an overview assessment will be carried out.

- An **overview assessment** looks in more depth at different aspects of your relative's daily life. A care manager will usually visit your relative's home. This may lead to the need for a further assessment, either by a specialist worker (specialist assessment) or a very detailed assessment (comprehensive assessment).

- A **specialist assessment** is carried out by a specialist worker, such as an occupational therapist, who may assess your relative's need for specialist equipment or alterations to his or her home.

- A **comprehensive assessment** is a very detailed assessment, which requires input from a number of other workers, maybe from the NHS, housing and voluntary organisations.

In Scotland, the Single Shared Assessment Process sets out four types of assessment – simple assessment, comprehensive assessment, specialist assessment and self-assessment. More information is available from the Scottish Executive on www.scotland.gov.uk/topics/Health/care/JointFuture/SSA.

Areas covered during the needs assessment

During the needs assessment, different areas of your relative's life should be considered. These areas are:

- Your relative's views (his or her problems and expectations).
- Clinical background (any medical problems, medication or any falls).
- Disease prevention (blood pressure, weight, drinking/smoking).
- Personal care and physical wellbeing (your relative's ability to look after him- or herself, any mobility difficulties or continence problems).
- Senses (any sight or hearing problems that are causing difficulties).
- Mental health (memory problems or depression).
- Relationships (family, friends, carer).
- Safety (difficulties relating to your relative's safety or the safety of others, neglect or abuse).
- Your relative's immediate environment and resources (whether your relative can look after his or her home, suitability of accommodation, benefit advice, ability to shop).
- Lifestyle choices (where your relative wants to live, any important interests).

PRIORITY LEVELS

In England and Wales, there are four priority levels for the help that councils can provide for your relative. These are outlined in the Fair Access to Care Services (FACS), which is a framework provided by the Department of Health in England to councils for setting eligibility criteria for adult social care. FACS advises councils to prioritise the needs of people according to the immediate and longer-term risk to them if their needs are not met. FACS also gives local councils discretion over the level of need and risk they meet. The level of need that each council meets is decided by local councillors and depends on the council's resources.

Critical need

These are the most serious and extreme circumstances. There may be a risk to life and/or a high risk that the person will not be able to remain in his or her current accommodation. Such people, due to their condition, may be unable to protect themselves from the risk of serious accident or harm, including self-harm. Support is needed to prevent the development of an avoidable health condition or to prevent such a condition becoming worse. There may be a risk where even the most basic essential tasks cannot be carried out. This may be an immediate problem or one very likely to occur without urgent intervention. Critical need is when one or more of the following occur:

- Life is, or will be threatened; and/or
- Significant health problems have developed or will develop; and/or
- There is, or will be, little or no choice and control over vital aspects of the immediate environment; and/or
- Serious abuse or neglect has occurred or will occur; and/or

- There is, or will be, an inability to carry out vital personal care or domestic routines; and/or
- Vital involvement in work, education or learning cannot or will not be sustained; and/or
- Vital social support systems and relationships cannot or will not be sustained; and/or
- Vital family and other social roles and responsibilities cannot or will not be undertaken.

Substantial need

These are circumstances where there is a significant level of need and the majority of normal day-to-day activities are affected. There is a substantial risk to the person or others now or in the foreseeable future and without the provision of support a critical risk will develop. Substantial need is when:

- There is, or will be, only partial choice and control over the immediate environment; and/or
- Abuse and neglect has occurred, or will occur; and/or
- There is, or will be, an inability to carry out the majority of personal and domestic routines; and/or
- Involvement in many aspects of work, education or learning cannot, or will not, be sustained; and/or
- The majority of social support systems and relationships cannot or will not be sustained; and/or
- The majority of family and other social roles and responsibilities cannot or will not be undertaken.

Moderate need

Circumstances are described as being moderate need when they affect some normal day-to-day activities and cause some concern. Moderate need is when:

- There is, or will be, an inability to carry out several personal care or domestic routines; and/or
- Involvement in several aspects of work, education or learning cannot or will not be sustained; and/or
- Several social support systems and relationships cannot or will not be sustained; and/or
- Several family and other social roles and responsibilities cannot or will not be undertaken.

 Each local council decides which of the levels of need it has the resources to meet and in March 2008, the Commission for Social Care Inspection (CSCI) reported that in the coming year, 73 per cent of English local councils were expecting to provide services only to people whose needs were assessed as 'critical' or 'substantial'. CSCI also reported that four councils were currently supplying services only to people in the 'critical' level.

Low need

Although there may be areas of need and normal life is being affected, the majority of day-to-day activities are still possible and the person has most of the relevant support systems in place. Low need is when:

- There is or will be an inability to carry out one or two personal care or domestic routines; and/or
- Involvement in one or two aspects of work, education or learning cannot or will not be sustained; and/or
- One or two social support systems or relationships cannot or will not be sustained; and/or
- One or two family and other social roles and responsibilities cannot or will not be undertaken.

❝ You can help your relative prepare for his or her assessment by keeping a diary, listing tasks that are proving difficult and the help required. ❞

PREPARING FOR AN ASSESSMENT

There are many ways that you can help your relative prepare for his or her assessment:

- **Suggest that you both think in advance** about the things your relative wants to talk about during the assessment.
- **Encourage your relative to draw up a list of tasks** he or she finds difficult and the services they think may help them.
- **If your relative has 'good' and 'bad' days,** suggest that he or she keeps a diary for a few days. In this your relative can note the activities that can be sometimes managed as well as the ones that are always difficult. It is good to be positive, but do encourage your relative to be realistic about the help that is needed (even if he or she hates admitting it).
- **Your relative should not assume that the person carrying out the assessment knows about their needs,** so encourage your relative to give as much detail as possible.
- **If your relative has difficulty communicating** or if English is not his or her first language, make sure social services know this in advance so that they can bring an interpreter or specialist literature.

 To find out more about government guidance on setting and applying eligibility criteria for England see: www.dh.gov.uk/en/Publicationsandstatistics/Publications. For Wales: http://new.wales.gov.uk/publications/circular. For Scotland: www.scotland.gov.uk/topics/Health/care/JointFuture/Publications/Guidance.

Questions your relative should ask the care manager during the assessment

- Please explain the council's eligibility criteria.

- Will the relative who cares for me be part of my assessment?

- How long will I have to wait until I know whether I am eligible for services?

- How long will I have to wait before I see my care plan?

- How many people will visit me before my assessment is completed?

- Who will provide my services; for example, the council, a private company or a voluntary organisation?

- Can you tell me about alternative ways of meeting my needs?

- Will my health, housing and transport needs be included in my assessment?

- When will I know how much I have to pay?

- When will my services be reviewed?

- What will happen if I am not eligible for council-funded services?

- Will I receive a written copy of my assessment or my care plan – even if I am not eligible for council-funded services?

❝It is always worth making a note of questions to ask in advance of the assessment.❞

THE CARE PLAN

Once the council has decided that it should provide or arrange services for your relative, the care manager should draw up a written care plan and give a copy to your relative. The care plan needs to be sufficiently detailed to enable you and your relative to know what help is supposed to be provided. As a minimum it should contain:

- **A statement of your relative's needs,** including his or her physical, social, emotional, psychological, cultural and spiritual needs, such as the need to live near relatives so that visiting and support are easy or to have food that meets religious and dietary needs.
- **Details of how these needs will be met,** including the services that are being provided and contact details.
- **Details of any charges your relative** has been assessed to pay and whether a direct payment (see pages 77–8) has been agreed.

 It is very important that all your relative's assessed needs are noted on the care plan, because these are the needs that the council must meet. For example, if your relative was assessed as needing a care home in another area (perhaps to be close to family), this must be noted on the care plan.

- The support that carers and others, such as voluntary organisations, are willing to provide.
- A date when your relative's needs and the services will be reviewed (see page 46).

Some councils provide care plans that set out clearly who will provide each service, which organisation they work for, when they will arrive and leave and what tasks they will be doing. If your relative needs to know more about what help is being provided or arranged, the person who drew up the care plan can explain in more detail.

Getting the best care for your relative

The local council's duty towards your relative is to provide or arrange services that meet his or her assessed and agreed needs, including social and emotional needs. These needs can sometimes be met in different ways, perhaps by your relative receiving care at home or by direct payments (see page 77), or by moving into a care home.

Where care needs could be met equally well in different ways, the local council can legitimately offer the cheapest option. Some councils set a limit on the amount of care they will provide or arrange before suggesting your relative should move into a care home. However, the Government's FACS guidance reminds local councils to 'tailor services to each individual's circumstances and ... only use upper cost parameters for care packages as a guide'.

45

If a more expensive care package in your relative's own home could meet his or her needs in a way that a cheaper care home could not, the local council cannot insist that your relative accepts the cheaper option on the grounds of cost alone. If your relative is in this position, he or she or you should negotiate with the care manager during the assessment to ensure that it is your relative's needs that are looked at rather than what services are available (but may not be really suitable). Your relative should ask the care manager to look again at ways of meeting his or her assessed and agreed needs to see if it is possible to remain at home. This may include considering whether any equipment, modified clothing, such as replacing buttons with Velcro, or home delivery shopping could reduce the amount of care needed.

If your relative feels the care plan does not reflect his or her care needs or some amendments are needed, your relative should talk to the care manager. If the issue remains unresolved, consider making a complaint (see page 203). Otherwise, if your relative is happy with the care plan, he or she and the care manager should sign and date it and your relative should be given a copy.

Jargon buster

Duty social work team The duty team takes requests for social services help when there is no member of staff actively working with a particular older person

" The care manager is the first port of call if there are concerns. **"**

THE REVIEW

The care manager should arrange to review your relative's needs and the services he or she is receiving at least once a year. This is usually at home, but can be in a hospital, day centre or in a care home if that is more appropriate. It is similar to the initial assessment, but will also consider whether your relative's needs have changed and whether your relative is still eligible for services.

If your relative's situation changes in the meantime, you or your relative can ask for a review earlier. Contact either the member of staff who carried out the original assessment or the **duty social work team**.

Withdrawal of service

If the council decides, following a review, to withdraw or reduce the services your relative has been receiving, they should check that your relative is not left at serious physical risk even though he or she appears not to meet the council's current criteria.

They should also check whether your relative has previously been given any assurances about the duration of the service. If services are withdrawn or reduced, with or without a review, the local council must tell your relative about their right of appeal by using the complaints procedure (see pages 201–7).

Case Study — Mrs James

Mrs James was 89, lived in Glasgow and was very frail and forgetful, unable to get out of her house and having difficulty using the toilet. Her daughter Marianne lived next door and cared for her mother. Marianne's GP suggested that Marianne contact the local council social work department and ask them to assess her mother's needs. Marianne rang the telephone number she had been given and told the person who answered that her GP had suggested she contact them to get help for her mother. She said that her mother was frail and that she lived next door, but she got flustered and forgot to tell them about the difficulties with the toilet. The lady on the phone sounded busy and once she heard that Marianne cared for her mother, she said Mrs James did not fit the council's criteria and therefore they would not arrange an assessment. Marianne went back to her GP and explained what had happened. The GP asked her receptionist to write (on official notepaper) explaining Mrs James' needs in detail and gave Marianne a copy. Two days later the Social Work Department contacted Marianne and arranged to visit and assess her mother the next day. Mrs James was soon supplied with equipment to help her in the toilet, a carer came two days a week to relieve Marianne and arrangements were also made for Mrs James to go to a day centre once a week.

CARER'S ASSESSMENT

There are two types of carer:

- **Formal carers** are paid by the council, a care agency or private company.
- **Informal carers** are family, friends or neighbours providing care or supervision.

If you are an informal carer, you may be living with or away from your relative and you may be caring full time or combining work with caring.

Informal carers have a legal right to a carer's assessment, which enables you to talk to the local council about the help you need with caring; with maintaining your own health; and how to balance caring with work and family commitments. Other things that the carer's assessment should cover are described overleaf.

For information about finding a carer, see pages 63-5, which discusses agencies and private companies.

- **Your housing.** Whether you and the person you care for live together or separately; if any changes are needed.
- **Your health.** If you have health problems or are depressed or anxious.
- **Work/leisure.** Whether you have had to reduce your hours of work or give up leisure activities.
- **The time you spend on caring duties.** If you have to give help during the day or night or both, what help you have.
- **Your feelings.** Do you feel you have a choice about providing the care? You may feel you cannot go on, or only if you have more help.
- **Dealing with emergencies.** Whether you have made any arrangements to cope if you suddenly became ill.
- **The future.** Any concerns you have for yourself or your relative.

To request a carer's assessment, contact your relative's local council, either by phone or in writing. If you know the name of the care manager who is responsible for your relative's services, ask for him or her or ask for the duty team.

Timing of an assessment

A carer's assessment can be carried out at the same time as the assessment for the person you care for, or it can be carried out separately. The assessment may lead to services for your relative, such as a day centre or respite care, to relieve you as the carer, or to services to help you in your caring role, such as benefits advice or equipment to help lift and move your relative.

There is no time limit for how soon the carer's assessment should be carried out, although your local council should carry out an assessment within a 'reasonable' time.

The finances

There is no charge for a carer's assessment and the person you are caring for may be eligible for the Attendance Allowance (see page 34). If you as a carer are assessed as eligible for any services, such as a telephone, you are likely to be means tested.

❝ The assessment should include consideration of your feelings about whether you can go on giving care in this way. ❞

For more information about allowances, see Attendance Allowance (page 34), and the Carer's Allowance and the Carer Premium (page 36). More information about means tests is in chapter 4.

Staying at home

Most people want to stay in their own homes for as long as possible, even if they become frail and need help and support to retain their independence. This chapter describes the wide range of community-based services that can be provided or arranged by local councils, the NHS, not-for-profit organisations and commercial companies.

Helping your relative

If your relative has decided that he or she wants to stay at home but is finding it difficult to manage or you are concerned about his or her safety, there are various ways in which you can help.

PRACTICAL SUPPORT

- **Check your relative's finances.** Make sure he or she is claiming all the financial benefits to which he or she is entitled. For information on the State Pension and benefits, see pages 26–36. See also the websites listed in Useful Addresses (pages 211–14). For advice on managing money, such as private pensions and savings, talk to a financial adviser.
- **Check your relative's health.** Encourage your relative to contact his or her GP to ask for a check-up or advice on health conditions. Arrange for an emergency alarm to be installed to allow your relative to call for help 24 hours a day if he or she has an accident or is unwell (see page 60).
- **Check your relative's housing.** Talk to your relative about his or her housing. If he or she is worried about maintenance, such as broken windows, or the need for repairs, help him or her arrange for it to be done or contact the landlord, local council housing department or a local home improvement agency (see page 85). If your relative is also finding it difficult to get in and out of the house, perhaps because of high steps, contact the local council and ask for a needs assessment (see pages 38–43). If your relative owns his or her own home, you may want to discuss selling and moving somewhere smaller and easier to manage.
- **Crime prevention.** Contact the local police station and ask for a visit from the Crime Prevention Officer. He or she will be able to give your relative free advice about home security and may be able to arrange for your relative to have extra security fittings such as window locks. Contact the local police station, Age Concern, CAB or a local advice centre for further information (see box opposite).

❝ You can help give your relative practical support by checking his or her finances, health and housing, among other things. ❞

- If you become aware that your relative would like more social contact, get in touch with a local advice centre, Council for Voluntary Service (CVS) (your local library will have details of the local CVS(s)), Age Concern or the library to find out about local clubs and societies. Local branches of national organisations may also be able to offer support with specific problems, such as how to best manage with poor sight.

- If your relative needs help with activities such as preparing meals, dressing, shopping or if he or she needs equipment, such as a grab rail or a stair lift, contact the local council to ask for a needs assessment (see pages 26–36). If your relative does not fit the council's eligibility criteria, does not want to approach the council or does not want an assessment, all these and other services are available commercially (see page 57).

TO STAY OR MOVE?

Most older people want to continue living in their own home. The home often holds many memories of family life, the area is familiar and your relative will often have local friends on whom he or she relies for support and social contacts. But areas change, small shops disappear, friends move away and people's needs change as they get older and less mobile. Your relative may want to start thinking about a move to somewhere smaller, less expensive, more manageable, perhaps in a safer area or near family.

&&Most older people want to stay living in their own home. But areas change and friends move and they may want to be nearer their family. &&

Websites to help you

Age Concern: www.ageconcern.org.uk (England), www.accymru.org.uk (Wales), www.ageconcernscotland.org (Scotland) and www.ageconcernni.org (Northern Ireland).

Citizens Advice Bureau (CAB): www.adviceguide.org.uk.

Financial Services Authority (FSA): www.fsa.gov.uk (use this website to check if an independent financial adviser is registered). To find an independent financial adviser: www.unbiased.co.uk.

Help the Aged: www.helptheaged.org.uk.

Neighbourhood Policing Team: www.neighbourhoodpolicing.co.uk (England and Wales), www.scotland.gov.uk (Scotland) and www.psni.police.uk (Northern Ireland) (to find your relative's local team).

To move or not to move?

The purpose of this questionnaire is to encourage your relative to think about the different aspects of his or her home and identify what works and what does not. It will help your relative decide whether he or she wants to make changes at home, find out about services that would make life easier or move to alternative accommodation. The questionnaire can be used in several ways. You may like to use it purely as a prompt for a general discussion with your relative and/or with other family members, talking about each topic as you get to it. Or you and your relative may each like to look at it separately, note any topics that are causing difficulties and then talk about the results. If you would like to use the ratings system, work on the basis that:

- 10 rates as 'perfect'
- 6 rates as 'just OK'
- 5 rates as 'not good'
- 1 rates as 'terrible'.

The ratings are only intended to help you and your relative compare how 'good' or 'bad' any particular aspect of your relative's home is so that you can prioritise the various aspects and decide what, if any, changes he or she wants to make.

66 You could use this questionnaire for a discussion, or look at it separately and discuss the results. 99

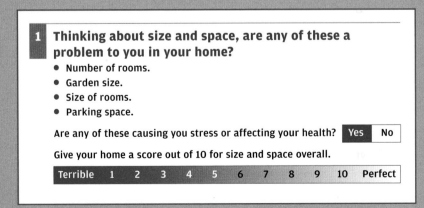

1 Thinking about size and space, are any of these a problem to you in your home?

- Number of rooms.
- Garden size.
- Size of rooms.
- Parking space.

Are any of these causing you stress or affecting your health?   Yes   No

Give your home a score out of 10 for size and space overall.

Terrible	1	2	3	4	5	6	7	8	9	10	Perfect

2 **Thinking about independence, are any of these a problem to you in your home?**

- Fear of eviction.
- Being too dependent on your family.
- Being unable to live as you please.
- Being unable to keep pets.
- Having to take too much responsibility for your home.

Are any of these causing you stress or affecting your health? **Yes** **No**

Give your home a rating between 1 and 10 for independence overall.

Terrible	1	2	3	4	5	6	7	8	9	10	Perfect

3 **Thinking about affordability, are any of these a problem to you in your home?**

- Paying the mortgage/rent.
- Paying for heating/hot water.
- Keeping up house maintenance.
- Paying the council tax.
- Paying house insurance.
- Paying the water bills.
- Paying service charges (for a flat).
- Paying for help in the home.

Are any of these causing you stress or affecting your health? **Yes** **No**

Give your home a rating between 1 and 10 for affordability overall.

Terrible	1	2	3	4	5	6	7	8	9	10	Perfect

4 **Thinking about the condition of your property, are any of these a problem to you in your home?**

- The roof or walls.
- Plumbing/drains.
- Plaster.
- Damp.
- Wiring.
- The windows/double glazing.
- The doors.
- The gas boiler/gas fire/gas fittings.
- Water supply.
- Garden fences.

Are any of these causing you stress or affecting your health? **Yes** **No**

Give your home a rating between 1 and 10 for the condition of the property overall.

Terrible	1	2	3	4	5	6	7	8	9	10	Perfect

To move or not to move? (continued)

5 **Thinking about comfort and design, are any of these a problem to you in your home?**
- It does not feel like home.
- It's too cold.
- It's too dark.
- Things aren't arranged as you wish.
- The decor.
- The furniture.

Are any of these causing you stress or affecting your health? **Yes** No

Give your home a rating between 1 and 10 for comfort and design overall.

Terrible	1	2	3	4	5	6	7	8	9	10	Perfect

6 **Thinking about security and safety, are any of these a problem to you in your home?**
- Hazards, such as worn carpets and slippery surfaces.
- The house is not secure if you are out.
- There is no help at hand in an emergency.
- The fire precautions are not good.
- You do not feel safe at home.
- You do not feel safe in the area.

Are any of these causing you stress or affecting your health? **Yes** No

Give your home a rating between 1 and 10 for security and safety overall.

Terrible	1	2	3	4	5	6	7	8	9	10	Perfect

7 **Thinking about location, are any of these a problem to you in your home?**
- It's not convenient for shops.
- It is too far from a bus or the bus service is poor.
- You are unfamiliar with/dislike the area.
- It is too noisy and stressful.
- It is too far from family/friends.
- You have problem neighbours.
- It is too far from key facilities.

Are any of these causing you stress or affecting your health? **Yes** No

Give your home a rating between 1 and 10 for location overall.

Terrible	1	2	3	4	5	6	7	8	9	10	Perfect

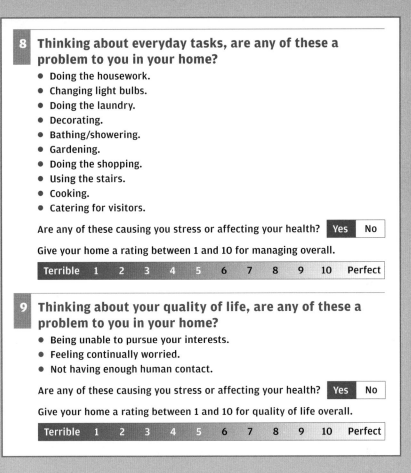

8 **Thinking about everyday tasks, are any of these a problem to you in your home?**
- Doing the housework.
- Changing light bulbs.
- Doing the laundry.
- Decorating.
- Bathing/showering.
- Gardening.
- Doing the shopping.
- Using the stairs.
- Cooking.
- Catering for visitors.

Are any of these causing you stress or affecting your health? **Yes** **No**

Give your home a rating between 1 and 10 for managing overall.

Terrible	1	2	3	4	5	6	7	8	9	10	Perfect

9 **Thinking about your quality of life, are any of these a problem to you in your home?**
- Being unable to pursue your interests.
- Feeling continually worried.
- Not having enough human contact.

Are any of these causing you stress or affecting your health? **Yes** **No**

Give your home a rating between 1 and 10 for quality of life overall.

Terrible	1	2	3	4	5	6	7	8	9	10	Perfect

❝ Think about the comfort and design of your home, together with its security and safety and the suitability of its location. ❞

Working through the questionnaire will help your relative decide whether he or she wants to move or make changes to their current home. Either way, your relative will need more information.

- To explore the possibility of making alterations to his or her home, the local council's needs assessment is the first port of call (see pages 38–46).
- If your relative wants to explore the possibility of moving, either to ordinary housing, retirement housing or to live with a relative, there is more information in chapter 5.

What support is available?

There are lots of different types of support available to help your relative stay at home if that is what he or she wants to do. This section looks at equipment, house alterations, alarm systems and services such as personal carers, meals and transport.

EQUIPMENT TO HELP MAINTAIN INDEPENDENCE

Equipment to help retain independence, for example, blocks to make chairs higher and therefore easier to get in and out of, raised toilet seats and frames, lifting seats and portable ramps, may be available from your relative's local council.

Before supplying equipment, however, the local council will need to have undertaken the needs assessment (see pages 38–46) to ensure your relative meets the eligibility criteria. This will obviously take time and, in addition,

Where to go for equipment

The Disabled Living Foundation is a national charity that provides free, impartial advice about all types of disability equipment and mobility products. It also produces fact sheets, including one with details of publications that carry advertisements for second-hand equipment. To find out more, go to www.dlf.org.uk.

Disabled Living Centres provide permanent exhibitions of products and equipment that your relative can try with advice and guidance from staff. There are over 50 Disabled Living Centres throughout the UK. To find your relative's nearest centre, go to www.assist-uk.org/centres.

The Disability Register: www.disabreg.pwp.blueyonder.co.uk, which has a magazine that lists second-hand equipment both for sale and wanted.

Ricability (the trading name of the Research Institute for Consumer Affairs, RICA): www.ricability.org.uk, researches and publishes independent information about a variety of disability equipment such as household products and mobility equipment.

Online shopping: Lloyds Pharmacy (www.lloydspharmacy.com) and Boots (www.boots.com) have high street stores and an online shop selling disability equipment. Keep Able (www.keepable.co.uk) and Nottingham Rehab (www.nrs-uk.co.uk) both have mail order catalogues and an online shop.

many councils do not now supply small items of equipment, such as pick-up sticks or tap turners. So if these are needed, you may have to look into purchasing at least the smaller items. There are various ways to do this:

- **Buying equipment privately.** All equipment is available for purchase from commercial companies, either through mail order catalogues or shops or showrooms. Some of the larger high street chemists stock smaller items of equipment, such as incontinence equipment, pick-up sticks and bath seats.
- **Buying secondhand.** Advertisements for second-hand equipment can be found in local and specialist papers.

For equipment and services to meet health-related needs, see pages 58–9.

Buying equipment privately

If your relative is thinking of buying equipment privately, there are some points that you both may want to consider:

- **Always try to get independent or professional advice when choosing equipment,** especially for large/expensive items such as stair lifts, scooters or hydraulic bath equipment. Obtain advice from

occupational therapists or physiotherapists working in hospitals or at the local council as well as the organisations listed in the box, left.
- **Make sure the products you buy comply with the relevant British Standards.**
- **Make sure the equipment is easy to use,** that appropriate and clear instructions are included and that your relative knows how to use the equipment correctly and is confident in its use.
- **Before purchasing (for example, if looking at bathing equipment),** ask the supplier if they can arrange for your relative to try it at home.
- **If you need to transport the equipment,** for example, a wheelchair, check whether it folds, if it fits in the car and if there is enough space to store the equipment at home.
- **Check maintenance and repair arrangements,** whether it needs to be serviced regularly, the cost, whether it is possible to get spare parts and whether there is a guarantee.
- **Check the company's returns policy,** for example, if your relative does not need the equipment any more. Some companies will subsequently arrange to buy back any equipment that is no longer needed.
- **Consider getting insurance for larger items,** such as a scooter.

 For more information about getting the best insurance deals, see the *Which? Essential Guide: Money Saving Handbook.*

Equipment and services to meet health-related needs

Some services and equipment are available to meet your relative's health needs. To find out more about the services described below ask at your relative's GP's surgery. Sometimes if the GP or nurse thinks your relative needs a more detailed assessment, he or she may suggest you approach your relative's local council for a needs assessment.

Chiropody

To be eligible for free NHS chiropody (often called podiatry) service your relative must have a referral from their GP's practice. Each person is assessed individually and treatment provided for 'priority cases', which depends on the seriousness of the condition and the risk factor. If free NHS podiatry is not available, your relative's GP can refer him or her to a private clinic for treatment but there will be a charge. You can also look in your relative's phone book for private podiatrists.

Communication equipment

Communication equipment for people who have limited or difficult to understand speech is supplied following an assessment by a speech and language therapist usually working in the speech and language centre of a hospital or other specialist clinic. The equipment can be either supplied on loan from the hospital or purchased and the speech and language therapist will be able to advise on sources of supply and funding.

Continence services

A continence adviser is usually an experienced nurse who can assess, advise and, if necessary, supply equipment. Your relative's GP will also advise or refer him or her on for more specialist help and advice.

Hearing aids

If your relative has a problem with hearing, his or her GP will first check whether there is a medical reason, such as an ear infection. If not, your relative will be referred to the local hospital for a hearing test and, if necessary, staff will discuss the options, which may include a hearing aid. Hearing aids are prescribed free of charge and are available for as long as they are needed or are useful. They can also be purchased privately and cost between £300 and £2,500. If your relative is thinking of buying a hearing aid, look at the Royal National Institute for Deaf People (RNID) fact sheet 'Buying a hearing aid privately'.

Home nursing equipment

This type of equipment includes items such as pressure relief mattresses, shower chairs, raised toilet seats and commodes. It can be available through the NHS as part of the local Primary Care Trust's hospital discharge schemes. Home nursing equipment is also available on short-term loan from the Red Cross where donations are welcomed.

Low vision aids, including magnifiers and talking clocks

These are usually supplied on loan following a recommendation from a hospital eye department. They can also be purchased privately: basic magnifiers can be found for under £20, complex models considerably more. For more details, contact the Royal National Institute of Blind People (RNIB).

Medication support

Speak to the pharmacist if your relative needs help with taking medicines, reading labels or opening packaging. The pharmacist may be able to replace the tablets with a syrup, put the tablets in easy-to-use containers and use large, easy-to-read labels. Some pharmacists run a prescription collection service, a repeat prescription service or a home delivery service.

Walking equipment, such as walking frames and trolleys

If your relative needs walking equipment, his or her GP or community nurse should arrange for a physiotherapist to assess your relative's needs and also teach him or her how to use the equipment correctly. If your relative is thinking of buying equipment, read the fact sheet 'Choosing walking equipment', available from the Disabled Living Foundation.

Wheelchairs

These are supplied by a local NHS wheelchair centre, each of which uses its own criteria when assessing. Wheelchairs are supplied free of charge on permanent loan and the centre will arrange repairs unless the fault was caused by misuse or neglect of the chair. Sometimes vouchers are offered to be put towards the cost of a wheelchair that is more expensive than the one the NHS would provide. For details about the wheelchair service, including contact details for local centres, go to NHS Direct. Wheelchairs can also be hired for days out or other short periods from the Red Cross.

Contact details

Any of the equipment and services mentioned can be organised through your relative's GP or community nurse. You can also go to:

Disabled Living Foundation: www.dlf.org.uk

NHS Direct: www.nhsdirect.nhs.uk; in Scotland: www.nhs24.com; in Northern Ireland: www.n-i.nhs.uk

Red Cross: www.redcross.org.uk

Royal National Institute of Blind People (RNIB): www.rnib.org.uk

Royal National Institute for Deaf People (RNID): www.rnid.org.uk

For further information, see Useful Addresses on pages 211–14.

ALARM SYSTEMS

An emergency alarm (also known as a community alarm or social alarm) can give your relative the confidence to continue living at home independently, knowing that help is at hand if needed. Emergency alarms work through the telephone and can be activated from anywhere in the home by pulling a cord (there could be a cord in each room) or by pressing a button on a neck pendant or wristband.

The alarm is linked to a call-monitoring centre that operates 24 hours a day, seven days a week. The monitoring centre knows the address from which the call has come and, depending on the alarm system, either speaks to your relative or alerts a neighbour, family or the emergency services.

Alarm systems are provided by local councils, charities and commercial companies. Each council has their own service and some provide alarms free of charge if your relative meets certain criteria, while others charge from between about £150 to £300 a year.

Telecare: These are more sophisticated alarm systems. They include sensors to detect whether water or gas has been left on, wandering alarms and sensors that alert to changes in routine; for example, if the bathroom is not used all day.

Things to consider when choosing an alarm system

- Make sure the neck pendant or wrist band is comfortable to wear, easy to use and check whether it will set off the alarm from anywhere in the home or garden.
- Find out if the pendant or wristband is substantial enough to withstand dropping. It is worth checking whether the product is compliant with BS EN 50134 (the European standard for social alarm systems).
- Ask whether the alarm unit allows your relative to speak and listen to the call-monitoring centre.
- Check that the button is easy to see and to use in an emergency and that the battery back-up power lasts at least 8 hours.
- Ask if the alarm automatically sends a low battery warning to the call-monitoring centre and who is responsible for replacing the batteries.
- The call-monitoring centre should be a member of Telecare Services Association (TSA). Ask if the service is available 24 hours a day, 365 days a year; whether there are at least two operators at all times to answer calls, and what arrangements there are to allow the call centre to continue to work if the telephone or electricity fail.

 Contact your relative's local council for details of their alarm systems. Alternatively, contact Age Concern (www.aidcall-alarms.co.uk) or Help the Aged (www.helptheaged. org.uk) (their service is called SeniorLink in England, Wales and Scotland, or CareLine in Northern Ireland). Both charities have a number of payment options.

- Check that information about service users is handled confidentially and that there are procedures to ensure operators provide appropriate assistance in a wide range of circumstances.
- If the call-monitoring centre holds keys to your relative's home, check that they are kept securely and identified only by code.

ALTERATIONS FOR YOUR RELATIVE'S HOME

If your relative is finding it difficult to manage at home because it is unsuitable, he or she may be eligible for help from the local council to make his or her home safer and more comfortable. Further details are given on pages 82–92.

DAY CENTRES

Some councils run day centres where your relative can go for a day or part of a day, to meet other people, share a meal and get involved in activities. Most provide door-to-door transport if your relative needs it. Some day centres provide services for people with specialist needs, such as dementia, or breaks for carers. In some areas, day centres are run by voluntary organisations such as Age Concern.

Your relative is likely to have to be assessed by the council before he or she is able to attend a council-run or council-subsidised day centre. Some voluntary organisations that run day centres will also assess your relative's needs before offering him or her a place. There is likely to be a charge for transport, meals and sometimes attendance. Contact your relative's local council for details of services and charges in their area.

PERSONAL CARE

Personal care includes activities such as getting up in the mornings, going to bed at night, using the toilet and washing yourself. The local council is the main provider of help with personal care, either by directly employing staff or by commissioning commercial or not-for-profit agencies to carry it out on their behalf. If your relative needs help of this sort, the council's need assessment should be your first port of call.

If your relative doesn't meet the council's eligibility criteria or he or she does not wish to contact the council, care can also be purchased privately from a care agency, which may be commercial or not for profit (such as a housing association). The care period can last for as long or short a period as is needed (from one hour a week to live-in care).

> **❝ Most personal care is provided through the local council. ❞**

 Contact the TSA at www.asap-uk.org to see their Code of Practice and for information about alarms and Telecare services.

Questions to ask a care agency

- Can the agency provide the care my relative needs?

- How will they match the most suitable worker to my relative's needs?

- What sort of training do the carers receive?

- What will happen if my relative's regular carer is off sick?

- What insurance does the agency have?

- What proportion of the care workers and managers have a National Vocational Qualification (NVQ) or Scottish Vocational Qualification (SVQ)?

- Does the agency have a standard contract that it uses for its work with private clients?

- What are the agency's charges, including weekend and bank holidays, and is there a minimum charge?

- How is payment required – by cheque, direct debit or some other way?

- Are there are any hidden extra charges? The prices quoted usually include national insurance contributions, travel and any VAT that is payable.

- What procedures does the agency have to:
  - Protect my relative from accidents, abuse, neglect or self-harm?
  - Cover the way staff handle my relative's money if the carer shops or pay bills?
  - Instruct staff not to borrow or lend money, not to accept gifts and not take children or pets into my relative's house without permission?
  - Ensure staff know what to do if they cannot get into my relative's home or if my relative has an accident?
  - Keep written records of the care that has been given and accurate timesheets for my relative to sign?

Finding a care agency

When choosing an agency:

- **Get a list of agencies in your relative's area.** This will be available from the local council, the social care registration authority or the United Kingdom Homecare Association (UKHCA).
- **Draw up a shortlist of agencies** that appear to be able to meet your relative's needs.
- **Check they are each a member of the United Kingdom Homecare Association (UKHCA)** as these agencies are required to adhere to their Code of Practice to ensure that high standards of care are provided.
- **Check they are each registered with the appropriate social care registration authority** (see below) and get their inspection reports and, if available, their star ratings.
- **Ask for their Statement of Purpose and price list.**
- **Ensure there is a clear agreement** between the agency and your relative about the type of care needed and the hours to be worked.

❝ You should know the type of care needed and the hours required. ❞

If your relative doesn't have a needs assessment

If your relative employs a carer privately from an agency (without having an assessment from the council), the agency should carry out an assessment of your relative's needs. This should include:

- **The help your relative needs** and details of any illness and medication.
- **Who else is involved** in supporting your relative.
- **Your relative's ability** to see, hear and communicate and his or her preferred method of communicating.
- **Any problems with continence** or mobility and any equipment your relative uses.
- **Arrangements for getting access** to your relative's house.
- **Any dietary requirements** and preferences and any religious and cultural needs.
- **Whether your relative** is at risk living at home.

Employing a carer

If your relative is employing his or her own carer(s) or personal assistant(s), perhaps through direct payments (see page 77), both need to know exactly what their responsibilities are and what to do if things go wrong. Things your relative should think of in this situation are described overleaf.

To check that an agency is registered and to view inspection reports, go to www.csci.org.uk (England); www.csiw.wales.gov.uk (Wales); www.carecommission.com (Scotland) and www.rqia.org.uk (Northern Ireland). To find about more about UKHCA and its Code of Practice, go to www.ukhca.co.uk.

- **Prepare a job description** with details of the carer's specific duties.
- **Prepare a set of disciplinary** and dismissal procedures and practices.
- **Draw up a contract** for his or her carer. This should include details of the rates of pay (including weekends and bank holidays), hours of work, probationary period, holidays and sickness. The job description and disciplinary procedures should form part of the contract (see pages 196–200).

 If advertising in a shop window or paper, never put your or your relative's full address. It is advisable also only to use the first part of the postcode and a PO box number or advertisement number. You should also request and take up references.

Personal care in Scotland and Northern Ireland

In Scotland

If your relative is 65 and over and lives in Scotland, he or she will not have to pay for personal care services provided by the local council. However, your relative may have to pay for cleaning and general home helps – this will be determined by a needs assessment. The local council should provide details of its charging policy. Personal care in Scotland includes help with washing, bathing, dressing and with mobility problems.

In Northern Ireland

If your relative lives in Northern Ireland and is 75 or over, he or she should not be charged for 'home help' services. Home help service includes:

- Basic household tasks, preparing and cooking food and shopping.
- Some personal and social care duties, such as help with washing, dressing and going to the toilet.

If your relative is under 75, his or her finances will be assessed by the local council to see how much he or she should contribute.

 For more information on personal care in Scotland, go to www.scotland.gov.uk. For Northern Ireland, go to www.onlineni.net or www.helptheaged.org. For sample contracts and disciplinary and grievance procedures that can be downloaded, go to www.ncil.org.uk.

- Carry out a basic health and safety check to ensure there are no hazards, such as loose rugs or faulty electrical goods at home.
- Be aware that he or she must pay the carer the statutory minimum for the hours he or she works.

Getting home help and domestic assistance

Many councils now concentrate their limited resources on people who need help with personal care and therefore no longer provide help with housework. You may want to ask the council what services they provide, and also ask your relative's local Age Concern whether they know of any local domestic services.

Laundry

A few local councils offer a laundry service for people who are incontinent or who cannot manage laundry for any other reason. Contact your relative's local council to ask if they can offer this service and how much it costs.

HOMESHARE

Homeshare is an international charity providing a simple way of helping people to help each other. A Homeshare involves two people with different sets of needs, both of whom also have something to offer each other.

- The householder, who has a home he or she is willing to share and is also in need of some help and support.
- The homesharer, who needs accommodation and is willing to give some help in exchange for somewhere to stay.

By putting these two people together, Homeshare finds the householder the help, support and security he or she needs. At the same time, the homesharer has a rent-free place to call home. Both people, their families and communities benefit from the arrangement and the costs are very low.

There are currently five Homeshare programmes in the UK and work is underway to develop more of them.

MEALS SERVICE

Each local council has its own arrangements to supply meals to people who have no other way of getting a meal. In a few areas, the service is run by the Women's Royal Voluntary Service (WRVS) or Age Concern on behalf of the council. Some councils run a meals-on-wheels service, while others deliver frozen meals and provide a small freezer, microwave or steamer for heating them. Occasionally the service operates seven days a week for those that need it, but more often it will be available up to five

 For more information about setting up a Homeshare programme in your area or about existing Homeshare programmes in the UK and around the world go to www.homeshare.org.

days a week. Special diets, such as diabetic, vegetarian or vegan, may also be available.

Most councils have eligibility criteria for supplying this service. An example is that the recipient has no other realistic way of getting a meal. Costs vary and are usually between £2 and £4 a meal, but a number of councils operate a means test. Contact your relative's local council for details of the criteria, availability of the service and costs.

Frozen meals can also be purchased privately either through local outlets or through a UK wide service (see below).

Websites to help you

Wiltshire Farm Foods: go to www.wiltshirefarmfoods.com for details of their UK-wide service.
Eisemann: go to www.eismann.co.uk to check whether they can supply meals in your relative's area. See also www.oakhousefoods.co.uk and www.supreme-cuisine.co.uk.

> **❝ Most councils have eligibility criteria for supplying meals. ❞**

TRANSPORT

There are various services to help older people with their transport needs.

Concessionary bus pass

In England, a concessionary bus pass is available to all people aged 60 and over and provides free off-peak travel (usually after 9am or 9.30am Monday to Friday and all day at weekends and public holidays) on local buses in any part of England.

In some areas there are also concessions for rail travel. To apply, contact your relative's local council.

In Wales, people aged 60 and over are entitled to the free bus pass, which can be used at any time of the day, but is restricted to your local council area.

In Scotland, everyone aged 60 and over is entitled to free local bus travel and scheduled long-distance coach services at any time of the day.

In Northern Ireland, residents aged 65 and over are entitled to a Senior SmartPass, which gives them free travel in both Northern Ireland and the Republic of Ireland.

Blue Badge Scheme

This is a national scheme of parking concessions for some disabled people travelling either as drivers or passengers.

For more information about concessionary bus passes in England and Wales, go to www.direct.gov.uk and, for Scotland, go to www.transportscotland.gov.uk/concessionarytravel. For Northern Ireland, go to www.drdni.gov.uk/Senior_citizen_smartpass.

Badge holders are exempt from certain parking restrictions; for instance, they are allowed free parking at on-street meters and pay and display bays. Your relative will qualify for a Blue Badge if he or she:

- Receives the higher rate mobility component of Disability Living Allowance (see page 35); or
- Uses a motor vehicle supplied by a government health department; or
- Receives a War Pensioner's Mobility Supplement; or
- Drives a motor vehicle regularly, has a severe disability in both arms and is unable or finds it very difficult to operate all or some types of parking meter; or
- Is a registered blind person.

Your relative may also qualify for a Blue Badge if he or she has a permanent and substantial disability so is unable to walk or has considerable difficulty in walking. Your relative may be asked to answer a series of questions to enable the local council to decide whether he or she is eligible.

Further details can be obtained from your relative's local council or see below. Some local councils charge a £2 administration fee, payable at the time of issue.

Disabled parking bay

If your relative is a disabled driver and has difficulty parking close to his or her home, the local council may be able to provide him or her with a parking bay. Criteria vary, though; for example, some councils restrict the service to Blue Badge holders. Likewise, procedures vary between councils. Some offer the service free of charge, while others charge from £30 upwards, so contact your relative's local council for details.

Scooters and buggies

A wide range of scooters and buggies are now available for the elderly and disabled; some can be driven on the pavement and some on the road. Scooters and buggies have to be purchased privately as they are not available through the wheelchair service (see page 59). They vary in price from about £500 to £3,000 (depending on the speed they travel and the accessories that your relative chooses).

It is advisable to get independent advice from an organisation, such as the Disabled Living Foundation, before purchasing a scooter or buggy and to consider insurance. Items of equipment such as scooters can be sold without VAT, providing the person using the equipment is chronically sick or has a disabling condition and the product is

 For information about the Blue Badge Scheme and where Blue Badge parking bays are across the UK, go to www.direct.gov.uk. Information about the Blue Badge in Wales is on http://new.wales.gov.uk; in Scotland on www.scotland.gov.uk/Topics/Transport, and in Northern Ireland on www.roadsni.gov.uk/index/bluebadge.

being purchased to help him or her personally. Your relative will need to sign a VAT declaration form, which the retailer will supply.

Door-to-door transport services

There are a variety of schemes that may be of interest to your relative. Some of them are:

- **Dial-a-Ride.** These schemes provide accessible door-to-door transport for people who cannot use public transport. They often use minibuses with tail-lifts. Most Dial-a-Rides will only offer local journeys and will not carry out journeys for which local council or NHS transport should be available, such as trips to hospital. There is often a mileage cost and sometimes a call-out charge, too. You can get more details from your relative's local council or the local Council for Voluntary Service or Age Concern.
- **Taxicard/token schemes.** These schemes are run by some councils for people who cannot use the bus service due to difficulties with access. They offer a number of concessionary journeys a year. Contact the local council to see whether there is a scheme in your relative's area.

- **Shopmobility schemes** lend powered wheelchairs and scooters to people who need them to shop, often in shopping precincts. All schemes operate slightly differently; some provide Shopmobility as a free service while others make a charge, so contact your local scheme. for more information (see box below).
- **Social car schemes.** These are small local schemes often using volunteer drivers. Their aim is to provide a local transport service for people who cannot use public transport. Contact the local council, Age Concern or advice centre for details of local schemes.

NATIONAL KEY SCHEME (NKS)

NKS was set up to allow independent entry by disabled key holders to accessible public toilets throughout the UK, many of which are locked to prevent vandalism. Keys can usually be purchased from the Royal Association for Disability and Rehabilitation (RADAR) (see box below), the local council, tourist office or disability group and cost about £3.50.

❝ There are various door-to-door transport schemes available. ❞

For details of Shopmobility schemes throughout the UK go to www.shopmobilityuk.org. To find out more about the NKS, go to www.radar.org.uk.

Living with family

If you are thinking about offering a home to an elderly relative, discuss the implications with the whole family and consider whether you all get on well together and have the same expectations. It is also useful to talk to someone outside the family who has been in a similar position.

THINKING IT THROUGH

Before going ahead, here are some things you may want to consider:

- **Some of the practicalities,** such as what will happen when you want to go away on holiday? Is there sufficient room for privacy and entertaining? Who will clean the house and do the washing? Will you eat together or separately?
- **Investigating to see if your relative will lose his or her entitlement** to means-tested benefits, such as Pension Credit, if he or she moves in with you.
- **If your relative were to put money into your home,** perhaps to build an extension or buy a larger property, you may want to consider what happens if:
  - The arrangement does not work out.
  - You need to move for employment, after retirement or other reasons.
  - Your relative needs to go into a care home and needs his or her equity to pay for care. Would you be able to re-mortgage or sell the property?
  - Your relative wants to leave some of his or her estate to other family members after their death.

LEGAL ARRANGEMENTS

Should you decide to go ahead with your plans, draw up a financial and legal agreement describing how you will deal with any disputes and terminate the arrangement if necessary. Also add your relative's name to the house deeds as owning whatever proportion of the property he or she has paid for (rather than specifying the amount of money that has been contributed).

MOVING IN WITH A RELATIVE

If you are thinking of moving in with an elderly relative to care for him or her, do think about your own future and particularly whether you will have security of tenure when your relative dies. Organisations that run telephone helplines, such as Age Concern, Help the Aged, Counsel and Care and EAC, regularly receive calls from a son or daughter who has moved in to the family home to care for an elderly parent, while other siblings live elsewhere. When the parent dies and the house is sold, the estate is often split equally among all the siblings. This can leave the caring sibling homeless and with too little money to buy another property.

Arranging respite care

Respite care is a short period of care, usually in a care home but sometimes at home with the help of paid carers. There may be a number of reasons for you and your relative to consider respite care; after a stay in hospital; to give the carers a break; to see whether your relative would like to live in the care home permanently or to have a holiday.

TYPES OF RESPITE CARE

There are several types of respite care for you or your relative to explore:

- **Convalescent homes.** In the past, people could go to a convalescent home to recover from an illness or stay in hospital. There are now very few of these traditional convalescent homes and they are mainly run by charities (see page 91–2).
- **Intermediate care.** Intermediate care covers a range of short-term rehabilitation services designed to help older people who no longer need hospital treatment but are not yet ready to return home. It can also be provided to avoid a hospital admission, for example, after a fall. Intermediate care services can be provided in your relative's own home or in a care home

and are usually limited to a maximum of six weeks. If the NHS has assessed your relative as needing intermediate care it will be provided free of charge by the NHS, whether in your relative's own home or in a care home. Intermediate care is a part of NHS Continuing Healthcare, which is discussed on pages 182–4.

- **Short-term care in a care home.** Short-term care can be provided in a care home offering personal care, such as accommodation, help with personal care, supervision and meals or in a nursing home offering care to people who are very frail, bedridden or who need a lot of attention from a nurse.
- **Care in your relative's own home.** It is sometimes possible to arrange respite care in your relative's own home. If your relative is not eligible for

To find out more about respite holidays, go to Holiday Care Service at www.holidaycare.org.uk, Vitalise at www.vitalise.org.uk.or and Tourism For All at www.tourismforall.org.uk.

intermediate care, he or she can pay carers to cover the time, for however long it is needed (for more information, see Personal care on page 61).

- **Holidays.** Some specially adapted hotels offer holiday/respite/short-term care for older people or people with disabilities, usually for a period of one or two weeks. Some of these hotels can arrange transport and may include outings and social activities.

❝ It may be possible to arrange respite care in your relative's own home. For holidays, some hotels offer special care for those with disabilities. ❞

ARRANGING RESPITE CARE

If your relative wants short-term care in a care home and will be paying the fees him- or herself, you or your relative should approach the care home, check the services they provide, whether they have a vacancy, the cost and whether they can offer the service your relative needs (especially if they have just come out of hospital).

If your relative needs help paying the fees, he or she should contact the local council and ask for a needs assessment and, if appropriate, an assessment of their carer's needs. If your relative is assessed as needing respite care, this will be noted on his or her care plan.

Paying for respite care in a care home

Once your relative has been assessed as needing respite care, he or she will have to pay for the care in one of two ways, depending on the council's policy. Either your relative will have to:

- **Pay a set rate,** which must be 'reasonable', to allow your relative to continue to pay for the upkeep of their home; or
- **The council will carry out a means test straight away.** After eight weeks of

For information about getting a needs assessment, see pages 38–46. For an assessment of a carer's needs, see pages 47–8.

respite care, the local council has to carry out a means test. Sometimes, older people receive regular respite care (perhaps one week in six). If this is the case with your relative and if the local council's policy is to charge a 'reasonable amount', this will be the amount your relative pays each time. The local council will not link any separate weeks together. If your relative is having a trial period in a care home, his or her Council Tax Benefit (see pages 31–3) and Housing Benefit can be paid by the council for up to 13 weeks.

If the temporary stay becomes permanent, the local council will carry out the means test under the normal rules (see page 74). But this assessment will only apply from the date a permanent stay was agreed.

Means test for people in respite care

When assessing for short-term care, the same upper and lower capital limits as for permanent care apply (see pages 167). For details of the means test for care homes, see pages 166–8.

** Sometimes older people receive regular respite care, perhaps one week in six.**

Case Study   Mr and Mrs Masterson

Mr and Mrs Masterson were both in their nineties, very frail and getting a little forgetful but living at home with support from family and neighbours. However, when Mr Masterson had to go into hospital as an emergency Mrs Masterson was not safe on her own at home. The GP contacted the intermediate care team who visited the same day and arranged for carers to visit four times a day to help Mrs Masterson get up, go to bed, take her medication and prepare and eat meals. Her daughter Gabrielle stayed with her mother for the first night and then arranged for a private carer to sleep in the house; she also rung her mother several times each day. The intermediate care was provided free of charge by the NHS and it enabled Mrs Masterson to stay safely at home for nearly three weeks, until her husband came home.

Funding care at home

Once it becomes apparent that your relative needs care – which could be because of a deterioration of health related to a medical condition, frailty or an event like a fall or a stroke – suddenly there will be a lot to think about and organise, in particular funding issues.

Paying for help at home

The type of care and support your relative may need to enable him or her to continue living independently could vary from major alterations to just having some help around the home. This section explains how the system works financially.

It is often the case that unless the care package services are being provided by the local council, a restricting factor could be what your relative can afford to purchase privately. In this chapter we look at how council funding works and the alternatives if your relative does not qualify for council support.

UNDERSTANDING THE SYSTEM

There are two stages to establishing how much funding might be available for your relative: these are the needs assessment (see pages 38–46) and the means test.

The means test

If, following an assessment of your relative's care needs, it is decided that he or she is in need of care and support by the local council, your relative will then normally undergo a means test (sometimes referred to as a financial assessment) to ascertain his or her financial position. The means test will look at both savings and income to assess how much your relative could contribute towards the cost. This process is discussed in greater detail on pages 75–8.

If the local council has assessed your relative as needing care in his or her own home, they can either provide it directly or arrange for it to be delivered through local commercial or not-for-profit agencies. They will then work out how much your relative should contribute towards the cost. Although local councils have the discretion as to whether to charge for home care services, in practice most will charge.

There is a national framework that provides guidance to local councils on how to work out charges for home care provided or arranged by them. This is called 'Fairer charging policies for home care and other non-residential social

The English version of 'Fairer charging policies for home care and other non-residential social services' can be downloaded from the Department of Health's website at www.dh.gov.uk and the Welsh version can be downloaded from www.wales.nhs.uk.

> ❗ Local councils should publish and make available to users and carers clear information about charges and how they are assessed. This information should be made available at the time a person's needs assessment is carried out and, after the means test, written information should be provided detailing how any charges are worked out and payable.

services'. England and Wales both use guidance of this name. In Scotland, personal care is free for those 65 and over, but charging still applies to non-personal care services, such as day care, luncheon clubs, meals on wheels and community alarms.

HOW THE MEANS TEST WORKS

In principle, the fairer charging policy is designed to give people a degree of financial security by allowing them to retain a minimum amount of money for their own personal use, rather than it all being used up paying for care. This amount is set as a 25 per cent buffer above the basic levels of the guaranteed credit of Pension Credit (see page 29).

For example, if your relative is receiving standard Pension Credit of £124.05 per week, 125 per cent of that would be £155.06 and this must be ignored in calculating the income assessable when charging for care.

If, however, your relative has capital or savings in excess of £22,250 (£22,000 in Wales), he or she can be charged the full cost of care. These are the minimum capital limits provided in the fairer charging guidance. Some local councils exercise their discretion by increasing them or set a maximum level of charges people should be expected to pay.

Some care is free

Care provided by the NHS, such as nursing services provided by community or district nurses, is free as is the first six weeks (four weeks in Scotland) of intermediate care. This is provided to prevent your relative from going into hospital or to support your relative if he or she has just been discharged from hospital.

Also, in England and Wales, if someone has been detained in hospital for assessment and treatment under sections 3, 37, 45A or 47 of the Mental Health Act 1983 aftercare services provided under section 117 of that same Act should be delivered free of charge. More information on section 117 aftercare can be found on www.mind.org.uk.

Varying charges

Local councils may charge differently depending on the services being used. For example:

- Meals at home or in a day centre may be charged at a flat rate to all users, without applying a means test because they are a substitute for ordinary living costs that your relative might be expected to incur.
- The charges for other services would be based on the number of hours of service provided. Whatever method is used, the charges must be deemed to be reasonable. Unlike for residential care, there is no published information about how much each council will charge for care services.

The benefits that can be taken into account are:

- The severe disability premium of Pension Credit.
- Attendance Allowance.
- Disability Living Allowance.
- Constant Attendance Allowance.
- Exceptionally Severe Disablement Allowance.

These will be taken into account as long as they do not reduce your relative's income below the 25 per cent buffer level or do not result in the user being left without the means to pay for other necessary care, support or other costs associated with their disability.

The local council should provide an individual assessment of disability-related expenditure before taking these benefits into account.

What isn't included in the means test

- The value of your relative's home.
- Rent/housing costs. The council will allow an amount for housing costs – either rent or mortgage payments and council tax. The amount they will normally allow is net of any Housing or Council Tax Benefit. Some councils may also allow deductions from income for water rates or charges and home insurance.
- The mobility component of Disability Living Allowance (see page 35).

Couples

If only one member of a couple requires care, the means test should only take into account the resources of that person. Any joint accounts are treated as divided equally between the partners. Therefore, if just one member of a couple needs

For information about Pension Credit, see page 29; for Attendance Allowance, see page 34; for Constant Attendance Allowance, see page 35 and for Exceptionally Severe Disablement Allowance, see page 35.

A typical local council assessment of income

Income (per week)		Amount
State Pension		£90.70
Private pension		£130.00
	Total income	**£220.70**
Deduct £124.05 plus 25%		(£155.06)
Deduct rent/housing costs		(£50.00)
	Total deductions	**(£205.06)**
Assessable income remaining, which could be a contribution towards the care costs		**£15.64**

care, it would be sensible to split any joint accounts into single accounts before the assessment so that the care is paid only from the account of the person needing it and thus reducing their capital only. The council will take into account the 'actual' amount of capital or savings held by the person who needs the care, therefore if joint accounts were split disproportionately, say 95/5 per cent, before there was any idea that care was going to be needed, then such a split should stand.

DIRECT PAYMENTS – CASH INSTEAD OF CARE

Direct payments are amounts of money paid by the local council direct to your relative and the payments are intended to enable him or her to arrange and buy in their choice of care. They are designed to give people greater freedom of choice over the care they receive and must be spent on meeting the assessed needs.

Your relative can choose to have some services provided or arranged by the council and use a direct payment for other services.

The local council must be satisfied that the way the money is spent is achieving this. For example, your relative can use it to employ his or her own care workers or use an agency. It cannot be used to pay a relative or anyone else living in the same household unless that person is specifically employed as a live-in carer, but it could be used, for example, to pay a neighbour for help in the garden. If your relative chooses to receive direct payments instead of care or support arranged by the local council, he or she has to keep a record of exactly how the money is being spent in meeting his or her assessed needs.

If, having accepted direct payments, your relative decides for any reason that he or she would prefer the council to arrange the care, then the payments can

Direct payments

- Direct payments can be used to pay for most community care services that the local council provides, except long-term residential care.
- Direct payments can only be offered to people who have been assessed as being eligible for specific services, they cannot be used to meet needs that social services are not prepared to meet.
- Your relative must be willing to have a direct payment and, either alone or with help, be able to manage the use of them in purchasing the services that are needed.
- Your relative will still be assessed as to what financial contribution he or she should make towards the cost of care and then use direct payments in the same way as if the local council was arranging or providing services.
- The local council remains responsible for monitoring and checking that your relative's needs have not changed.

be stopped and the services can be provided by the council instead. Similarly, if the council feels your relative is not managing with direct payments, they will take over.

CHALLENGING THE MEANS TEST

If your relative considers that he or she cannot afford what the local council says must be paid for their services, there is a process by which your relative can ask for a review of the charge. Each local council should make information available that makes it clear that users of services can either seek a review of their assessed charge, or can make a formal complaint if they are dissatisfied with any aspect of their assessment. Your relative should receive this information during the assessment process and it is discussed further on pages 203–4.

Individual budgets

Individual budgets (also called self-directed support) are designed to promote independence and choice for people receiving care or support. Individual budgets bring together a number of funding streams (for example, it could include a social services care package or direct payments with a Disabled Facilities Grant arranged through the housing department) and give users a full understanding of the finance that is available to enable them to make decisions about the care they receive. Individual budgets have been piloted and the government has announced its intention of rolling out the programme nationally. But at the time of writing, no specific details have been announced.

 To find out more about individual budgets go to http://individualbudgets.csip.org.uk or www.ncil.org.uk/individual-budgets.asp.

Paying for care privately

If the local council will not deliver the care your relative needs and he or she owns the home, a last resort could be for your relative to release equity from the property. This is becoming increasingly popular as older people have seen substantial increases in the value of their properties, but there are downsides to be aware of.

EQUITY RELEASE

Before considering equity release, your relative should consider possible alternative solutions, such as borrowing from family or friends, using existing savings or investments, looking into unclaimed benefit entitlement or grants or moving to a smaller property.

Equity release can be achieved through two different types of scheme: a lifetime mortgage and a home reversion plan.

A lifetime mortgage

This is based on raising a loan against the value of your relative's home that is repaid when he or she moves out or dies. The amount your relative can borrow depends on the value of the property, his or her age and, with some companies, health. Equity release is available to people aged 55 years plus; however, the older your relative is, the greater the cash sum that can be released. Most lenders will release a set percentage of the property's value based on the applicant's age. The amount available varies between lenders but, typically, a 60-year-old could release 20 per cent, a 65-year-old

25 per cent, and so on up to normally 55 per cent.

Unlike conventional mortgages, the interest rate can be fixed for life (it is currently around 6 per cent). This gives the peace of mind and certainty that the interest rate will never increase and your relative can project how much the debt would be over a number of years. As the interest is 'rolled up', the longer the plan exists the greater the debt will be. Most companies now offer negative equity guarantees so that the debt will never accumulate to more than the property is worth at the end of the tenancy (see below).

Early repayment charges

Because equity release plans are designed to be for life, early repayment charges may be applied if your relative wanted to end the plan early. The early repayment charges will vary depending on the lender and some may not levy a charge at all. They are usually based on a fixed percentage of the amount borrowed and would normally apply if the plan was ended voluntarily within the first 5-10 years.

A home reversion plan

With a plan like this, all or part of your relative's property is sold to a home reversion company in exchange for a cash lump sum, an income or both. Your relative will receive less than the full market value for the share of his or her home being sold. The amount that is discounted in exchange for a rent-free lifetime tenancy in the home reversion company's share of the property, could typically be between 35 and 60 per cent. The older your relative is when starting a plan, the greater the amount he or she receives.

 Equity release companies are regulated by the FSA so, if your relative has a complaint, he or she can take it up through them. Equity release providers should also be members of Safe Home Income Plans (SHIP), which is a voluntary organisation aimed at protecting the consumer and promoting safe home income and equity release plans. However, this doesn't always mean a company is 100 per cent reliable, so before taking out an equity release scheme, always consult an independent financial adviser (IFA) who is qualified to advise on equity release.

Points to consider before releasing equity

- Depending why the money is needed, it might be better to take a regular income or **drawdown** facility so that your relative is only paying interest on the money that is needed rather than taking a large lump sum, which will attract interest charges. Alternatively, a single lump sum might be released to purchase a care fee payment plan, which could deliver a regular income to pay for care.
- Taking out any form of equity release could adversely affect your relative's entitlement to means-tested benefits or support. The amount released may be treated as either capital or income in a means test. It may also be the case that your relative is already eligible for benefits which, if claimed, would give him or her sufficient income so as to avoid releasing equity.
- What grants or subsidised loans might be available (see pages 82–5) if your relative needs to raise capital for home alterations or necessary repairs or improvements.
- Negative equity guarantee. Members of SHIP guarantee that the amount repayable by anyone releasing equity from their property will never exceed the sale proceeds of the property. This is called a 'no negative equity

To find out more about SHIP and their Code of Practice, go to www.ship-ltd.org. You can find a local IFA by visiting www.unbiased.co.uk or calling 0800 085 3250.

guarantee' and without it, if property prices were to drastically fall, borrowers could find themselves owing the equity release company more than the property is worth. SHIP members display the SHIP logo in their brochures and other printed material as a guarantee to their customers.

- **What would happen if your relative wants to move house?** All SHIP-approved plans allow the plan to be transferred to a new property, providing it meets with the approval of the scheme provider. Few lenders would consider sheltered or retirement housing to fit their criteria, however. If your relative were downsizing and the

Jargon buster

Drawdown This is a facility to take the amounts of money you wish from an equity release scheme as you need it rather than in a lump sum

loan exceeded the lender's criteria because the new property was of less value, then they would allow a transfer of the plan except they would expect a proportion of the loan to be repaid from the proceeds. There would not normally be any early redemption charges in these circumstances.

The dos and don'ts of equity release

The dos

- Before releasing equity through one of these schemes, consider the alternative solutions that may be available to your relative (see page 79).
- Consider the impact any borrowing may have on your relative's entitlement to means-tested benefits or local council support. Means tests will take into account capital and income taken from equity release (see page 79).
- Involve family members in your decision. They may be able to assist with alternatives and it's helpful to keep them informed if they are also executors of your relative's estate.
- Ask as many questions as possible.
- Borrow only what is needed immediately. Using a drawdown plan means interest is only paid from the date the money is borrowed.

The don'ts

- Don't borrow money to invest. It is risky to hope that investing money borrowed would provide a return greater than the costs of borrowing it.
- Don't proceed without specialist advice. Choose an independent solicitor with experience in dealing with equity release and preferably agree a fixed fee. Also choose an independent financial adviser (IFA) with the relevant equity release qualification and experience and access to all equity release plans on the market.

Home alterations

In order for your relative to remain in his or her own home, perhaps with the support of a carer, it may be necessary to carry out some alterations, adaptations or necessary repairs to make the home more comfortable and suitable.

FUNDING

If your relative has sufficient savings, then paying for home alterations or adaptations may not be too much of a problem. Failing this, if he or she needs to raise money for such works, your relative may be eligible for a grant from the local council or a loan with more favourable terms from a body such as the Home Improvement Trust (HIT) (see box, opposite top). As a last resort, there are also equity release schemes, as discussed on pages 79–81.

Disabled facilities grants (DFG)

These are local council grants to help towards the cost of adapting people's homes to enable them to live more independently, safely or more comfortably. As part of the process, an occupational therapist will visit and assess what alterations are appropriate to meet your relative's needs. These may include:

- Widening doors and installing ramps.
- Providing or improving access to rooms and facilities, for example, by installing a stair lift or providing a downstairs bathroom.

- Improving or providing a heating system that is suitable for your relative's needs.
- Adapting heating or lighting controls to make them easier to use.
- Improving access to and movement around the home to enable your relative to care for another person who lives in the property, maybe their partner or a child.

The maximum amount of grant available is £25,000 per application in England and Northern Ireland and £30,000 in Wales, although local councils do have discretionary powers to increase the amount if the eligible works cost more. For grants in Scotland, see box on page 84.

" Your relative may be eligible for a grant from the local council or a loan with favourable terms from the Home Improvement Trust. "

The Home Improvement Trust (HIT)

HIT is a not-for-profit organisation that has links to a number of regulated banks and building societies to provide low-cost loans to older people for minor alterations or home improvements. HIT runs a scheme called 'Houseproud' working with local councils and home improvement agencies in England, Scotland and Wales. There is no similar organisation in Northern Ireland.

The means test

DFGs are normally assessed through a means test of the disabled person's and partner's average weekly income. Set allowances and premiums for outgoings are also taken into consideration.

A set housing allowance is used together with a range of premiums for degrees of disability and/or dependents and personal allowances, depending on your relative's age and whether he or she is single or a member of a couple. The assessment takes into account savings above £6,000, although certain benefits are generally ignored.

Depending on the outcome of this assessment, the amount of financial assistance offered varies from 0 to 100 per cent of the cost of the work. In general, if your relative's income is:

- **Less than his or her assessed outgoings,** your relative will not normally need to contribute to the cost of the works.

> **"** The amount of financial assistance offered varies from 0 to 100 per cent of the cost of the work. **"**

Eligibility

To be eligible for a DFG, your relative must be disabled and either the owner or tenant of the property and able to certify that he or she intends to occupy the property as his or her only or main residence throughout the grant period – currently five years. From April 2008, where the DFG is in excess of £5,000, the local authority can place a condition on the grant that provides a discretion for them to be able to reclaim up to a maximum of £10,000 if your relative were to sell or transfer the property within ten years.

 To find out more about the HIT, visit www.houseproud.org.uk.

- More than his or her assessed needs, a calculation is made to ascertain the size of loan. Your relative would have to pay a proportion of the costs, depending on the size of his or her income. If the loan amount is less than the cost of the works, the difference between the two is paid as a DFG (see page 32).

Funding through social services

In Northern Ireland and Wales, the local social services department can charge for any community equipment and alterations your relative might need. In England, as long as your relative has been assessed as needing it, any equipment or alterations costing less

---

Grants in Scotland and Northern Ireland

In Scotland, there are housing grants from the local council similar to DFGs in England and Wales. These are:

- A compulsory grant for providing basic amenities, such as a toilet.
- A minimum percentage grant, where the council pays half of the cost of some alterations.
- A discretionary home improvement grant where a disabled person can receive up to £20,000 to make the property suitable for his or her welfare needs. In order to qualify, the house must be your relative's private dwelling, not a second or holiday home, for a period of five years following the grant and, as far as possible, be kept in a good state of repair. In exceptional circumstances, the local council can apply to the Scottish Executive for an increase of the £20,000 limit.

For more information about what grants are available, see the Scottish Executive booklet 'Housing Grants' (go to www.scotland.gov.uk). Age Concern Scotland also produces a useful fact sheet, 'Older homeowners – financial help with repairs and adaptations'. Go to www.ageconcernscotland.org.uk.

In Northern Ireland, grants are available to help with the cost of the work:

- Disabled facilities grant, which covers works recommended by an occupational therapist up to a maximum of £25,000.
- Home repair assistance grant, which covers work relating to the external fabric and wiring of the property up to a maximum of £5,000 over three years.

These are subject to a means test called a 'test of resources' (TOR).

More information from www.nihe.gov.uk.

than £1,000 should be provided and fitted free of charge. These would typically include minor works or alterations such as ramps or grab rails. The assessment is normally carried out by an occupational therapist who will visit your relative and, once approved, the work is then carried out. The social services department can also help with:

- **Top-up funding** if your relative was not able to find the money to pay his or her assessed contribution to a DFG.
- **Covering the costs of work that is not covered by a DFG.** This provision varies considerably between councils.

Getting the work done

To apply for an alteration to your relative's home, contact the local council social services department, housing department or a local home improvement agency (HIA) (see box, below), or the local Housing Executive grants office if living in Northern Ireland.

❝Home improvement agencies help older, disabled and vulnerable homeowners or tenants to repair or adapt their homes.❞

Home improvement agencies (HIAs)

HIAs are not-for-profit organisations. In England, home improvement agencies are often called Care and Repair or Staying Put agencies. In Scotland and Wales they are usually called Care and Repair and, in Northern Ireland, they are known as Staying Put.

HIAs vary in size and facilities and are locally managed organisations. They help older, disabled and vulnerable homeowners or private tenants to repair, improve, maintain or adapt their homes.

Their services include guidance on how to get financial help to undertake the work, technical support in planning the work and making sure it is carried out by accredited tradespersons.

Most HIAs offer additional services such as handyperson schemes, gardening schemes and lists of approved contractors. The initial visit is free and charges for managing a project will always be discussed first and can usually be included in any grant that is given.

 To find your relative's local HIA go to www.foundations.uk.com (England); www.careandrepair.org.uk (Wales); www.careandrepairscotland.co.uk (Scotland) and www.nihe.gov.uk (Northern Ireland). You can find details of HIAs across the UK at www.HousingCare.org.

How long will it take?

Alterations are often large and complex building projects and they can take a long time to complete with several different agencies and staff involved. Unfortunately, there may be delays at any stage of the process. Your relative may have to wait for an OT assessment, to be allocated a worker from the HIA, the funding to be sorted out (including the grant application to be prepared, submitted and approved and your relative's assessed contribution to be found), planning permission to be gained (if needed), the work to be tendered, tenders to be accepted and building work to start. Be prepared for a complex project to take up to a couple of years to complete.

Case Study Mr Desai

Mr Desai was in his early seventies and lived with his wife, son and daughter-in-law and his two teenage grandchildren in the West Midlands. Mr Desai had had a recent neurological illness, which had left him confined to a wheelchair. He weighed 17 stone. The family lived in their own terraced house, which had a through room and kitchen downstairs and three bedrooms and a bathroom/toilet upstairs. Mr Desai had been assessed before leaving hospital and plans were made for him to return home with a bed and hoist in a curtained-off area of the living room and to use a commode in the kitchen, while ground floor facilities were built.

An occupational therapist visited Mr Desai at home, recommended a ground floor bedroom, shower and toilet and the case was passed to the local HIA, who supervised the work. However, the project encountered many difficulties:

- Mr Desai and his family wanted a two-storey extension to include an extra bedroom upstairs. This could not be funded through a disabled facilities grant (DFG) and no other funding was available.
- Planning permission was delayed while discussions continued with two neighbours who objected to the proposed extension.
- Mr Desai had difficulty in raising his assessed contribution to the DFG and after considerable negotiation the social services department contributed to the cost.
- Building work took longer than normal because there was no rear access to Mr Desai's house and a crane had to be used to move some of the building materials from the road to the site.

Mr Desai and his family coped remarkably well, but when things got too bad, he moved into a care home for a few weeks. The work was finally completed 26 months after the initial assessment.

Alterations in Scotland and Northern Ireland

In Scotland, the system for arranging alterations is substantially the same as for England and Wales. Application is to your relative's local council with assessment by an occupational therapist.

Advice and information about alterations for disabled people in Scotland is available from Care and Repair Forum Scotland at www.careandrepairscotland.co.uk. More information is available from http://scotland.shelter.org.uk.

In Northern Ireland, for people with tenancies in Housing Executive or housing association properties there is no charge for alterations and application should be made to the local district office of the Northern Ireland Housing Executive (NIHE). The process is very similar to that used in England and Wales, however, it will include an options appraisal during which NIHE staff will discuss all your relative's housing options, including a transfer to alternative accommodation. Homeowners or people living in privately rented homes should apply to their local Health and Social Services Trust. They will then be assessed by an occupational therapist and usually referred to the local Care and Repair.

More information for alterations in Northern Ireland is on www.nihe.gov.uk.

« Home adaptions can be large and complex projects involving many agencies, so they take time. Some take a couple of years to complete. »

WARM FRONT GRANTS

Warm Front grants are a government-funded initiative in England to make homes warmer and more energy efficient. The amounts payable are up to a maximum of £2,700 or, in the case of oil-fired central heating, £4,000 per home. Warm Front grants are available to all ages of qualifying householders receiving certain benefits. For older

For more information, call the Warm Front scheme manager on freephone 0800 316 6011, textphone 0800 072 0156 or apply online at www.warmfront.co.uk.

people aged over 60 years these would typically be:

- Council Tax Benefit, which must include a disability premium.
- Housing Benefit.
- Pension Credit.
- Disability Living Allowance.
- War Disablement Pension.
- Attendance Allowance.

The grant covers such work as loft insulation, cavity wall insulation or repairing and upgrading or installing new central heating systems. Your relative will need to complete an application form from Warm Front (see box on page 87) before a home energy adviser visits to assess and recommend any work for his or her property.

"Work such as loft and cavity wall insulation and improving or installing central heating might be covered by a grant."

THE SOCIAL FUND

Other help towards keeping your relative's home warm can come in the form of Cold Weather Payments or Winter Fuel Payments from the Social Fund through the Department of Work and Pensions (DWP) and, as such, are available across the UK. The Social Fund provides discretionary lump sum payments, grants and loans for important costs that people might find are hard to pay for out of their regular income.

Cold Weather Payments

A Cold Weather Payment is intended to help towards extra heating costs during very cold weather. This would be when the average temperature for an area is recorded as 0° Celsius (freezing point) or below over seven consecutive days. They are also made when the Meteorological Office forecasts such a spell of cold weather.

An amount of £8.50 per week during the cold weather spell is paid automatically along with other benefits your relative might receive. To qualify for a Cold Weather Payment, you relative must be getting Pension Credit or income-based Jobseeker's Allowance, which includes either a premium for being 60 or over, or one for being disabled or long-term sick. Your relative may also qualify if, which is unlikely in

For more information on the benefits listed above, see pages 29-35.

Winter Fuel Payment

A Winter Fuel Payment is an annual non-means-tested, tax-free payment made from the Social Fund to eligible people aged 60 or over to help towards their winter heating costs. It is not dependent on being eligible for any form of benefit. For more information, see page 36.

the case of older people, he or she is getting income-based Jobseeker's Allowance and has a child under the age of five or who is disabled.

Community Care grant

A Community Care grant might be available to your relative if he or she is in receipt of, or would be entitled to, income-based Jobseeker's Allowance or Pension Credit. In addition, your relative should be within six weeks of leaving institutional care or a care home providing a lot of care or supervision, for example, hospital, prison or a residential care or nursing homes. The payment is awarded for the purpose of easing the financial pressure of moving into the community and is non-repayable.

Grants may be awarded to people who are leaving accommodation in which they received care, to help people to settle or continue to live in the community. Grants can also be awarded to help ease exceptional pressures on families coping with someone needing care, or to help with certain travel costs. The minimum amount that can be awarded is £30, with separate arrangements for paying travelling expenses. The amount payable also depends on how much is in the Social Fund budget and how your relative's needs are prioritised against those of other applicants. The amount awarded will usually be affected if your relative has savings of more than £500, or £1,000 if your relative or partner (if he or she has one) is aged 60 or over.

❝Among other things, grants can be awarded to help ease pressures on families coping with someone needing care.❞

To find out more about the Social Fund and each of the payments and grants that are available, go to www.dwp.gov.uk/advisers/sb16.

Budgeting Loan

A Budgeting Loan again available if your relative is in receipt of income-based Jobseeker's Allowance or Pension Credit and is an interest-free loan intended to help spread the cost of certain one-off expenses over a longer period. The minimum amount of loan that can be awarded is £100 and it can help towards the cost of various items, such as things needed for or to improve the home, clothing and footwear, travelling expenses and certain debts. Unlike grants, though, Budgeting Loans have to be repaid. However, savings of more than £1,000 will usually affect how much your relative can borrow, or £2,000 if your relative or partner (if he or she has one) is aged 60 or over.

Crisis Loan

This loan may be available to anyone aged 16 or over, whether or not they get any benefit, who needs help to meet expenses in an emergency or because of a disaster. A loan must be the only way of preventing serious damage or risk to the health or safety of your relative or to his or her family. Crisis Loans are interest free but, again, have to be repaid. Any money your relative has available to him or her affects the awarding of the loan.

There is no minimum amount of loan, but the maximum debt that your relative could owe the Social Fund, including both Budgeting Loan and Crisis Loan debt, cannot be more than £1,500.

❝ Crisis Loans aim to help those in dire emergencies, whether or not they get benefits. ❞

Funeral Payments

This payment from the Social Fund is to help with the essential costs of a respectful funeral, which your relative or his or her partner is responsible for arranging.

The payment can cover various aspects of the funeral, including burial or cremation costs, necessary travel expenses and up to £700 of associated expenses. If there is money available from the estate of the deceased, this will be deducted from the payment. Any payment made may then be recovered from any money available from the deceased person's estate when it becomes available.

Funeral Payments are only available if your relative is receiving income-based Jobseeker's Allowance, Pension Credit, Working Tax Credit where a disability or severe disability element is included in the award, Child Tax Credit at a rate higher than the family element, which is paid if a child has certain disabilities, Housing Benefit or Council Tax Benefit.

HELP FROM NHS CONTINUING HEALTHCARE

The range, type and level of services to be arranged and funded by the NHS to meet continuing health needs are decided by assessment, but in principle, where required, the NHS is responsible for:

- Primary healthcare.
- Assessment involving doctors and registered nurses.
- Community health services.
- Healthcare equipment.
- Rehabilitation and recovery (where this forms part of an overall NHS package of care as distinct from intermediate care described on page 70).
- Respite healthcare.
- Specialist healthcare support.
- Palliative healthcare.
- Specialist transport services.

❝ The NHS is responsible for a wide variety of services aimed at meeting continuing healthcare needs. ❞

HELP FROM CHARITIES

Another source of funding that is often unexploited is that from charities or benevolent societies, such as the Civil Service Benevolent Fund or the Army Benevolent Fund, that are associated

For more information about NHS Continuing Healthcare, see pages 182-4.

91

with particular companies, trades or professions, armed services, religious groups, societies and unions or for people with specific conditions or disabilities.

If your relative or relative's partner (if he or she has one) worked in a particular trade or profession or is associated with any particular groups, it's worth checking to see if there is a related charity or benevolent fund that can assist him or her if necessary.

This source of charitable funding can help people in financial difficulty or with particular care needs that are not being met, often in the form of cash grants. The payments could be small periodic amounts or larger sums, for example, if required for home alterations.

To find out more about charities and benevolent societies that your relative might be able to apply to, contact Benevolence Today, which brings together a number of grant-giving benevolent societies, or the Association of Charity Officers which direct people to relevant charities and benevolent funds.

 If your relative is seeking financial advice, ensure that he or she goes to a specialist independent financial adviser (IFA). To find an IFA in your relative's area, go to www.unbiased.co.uk.

❝ There are many charities associated with particular companies, trades or professions and other groupings. ❞

 The websites for the army and civil service benevolent funds are: www.armybenfund.org and www.csbf.org.uk. The Benevolence Today website is www.benevolencetoday.org and that for the Association of Charity Officers is www.aco.uk.net.

Choosing the right housing

According to the Institute of Actuaries (2005), UK homeowners aged 65 and over hold £1,100 billion in unmortgaged equity. But many also have pensions that are worth less than they hoped. If your relative is in this position, financial and lifestyle considerations may prompt him or her to think about downsizing.

Retirement housing

If your relative has made the decision to move to somewhere that is smaller and easier to maintain, there are various options to consider and one of these is retirement housing. Once your relative has an idea of what he or she is looking for, you will both probably want to investigate what is available in the chosen area.

DOWNSIZING

The advantages of downsizing are that:

- It can release equity, which can be used to supplement a pension.
- It enables your relative to maintain a foot on the property ladder.
- A smaller property reduces running costs, housework and maintenance.
- The move could fit in with changes your relative wants to make to his or her lifestyle. For example, a location that meets your relative's current needs or is more secure; a smaller garden that allows more time for other interests.

Important points to consider about downsizing

- It is much easier to move, settle down and make new friends when you are younger, so try to encourage your relative not to leave it too late.
- Do not over-estimate the amount of capital that will be released. The cost of moving and setting up a new home can eat into the proceeds of the sale of a family home. According to the Woolwich's Cost of Moving Home Survey (2006), moving costs can exceed £12,000.

- If your relative is thinking of somewhere smaller, it may also be useful for him or her to think about how much space is needed, perhaps for hobbies or to accommodate family or visitors.
- If your relative is choosing a new location, he or she may want to check it out at different times of the year and think about how suitable it will be in the future, perhaps when he or she no longer wants to or can drive.
- When choosing a property, your relative may want to think about how suitable it would be in the future if his or her needs change. For example, a flat with a lift to the top floor or a house with a ground floor toilet are good options.

WHAT IS RETIREMENT HOUSING?

Retirement housing comes in many different forms so it can be useful to visit several schemes and talk to some of the people who live there, as well as the scheme manager, before finally deciding on a particular property.

Retirement housing is easily managed, age-exclusive housing with support available when needed. It is sometimes called sheltered housing, warden-assisted or warden-controlled housing, or (in the case of Abbeyfield Societies, see page 101) supported sheltered housing. Extra care housing is a form of retirement housing with meals, personal care and support available (see pages 104–6). There are over 25,000 retirement housing schemes throughout the UK providing around 600,000 homes for around 750,000 older people.

Most retirement housing has a scheme manager (previously known as a warden), an emergency alarm and some communal facilities. Retirement housing is usually built as a small development (often called a scheme) of between 15 and 60 self-contained properties, usually flats or bungalows, with one or two bedrooms. Most have special design features, such as level access, a lift and raised electrical sockets, and there are often communal facilities, such as residents' lounge(s), guest room and laundry. Meals are not normally provided, but some retirement housing can organise a hot meal once a day.

If your relative is interested in looking further into retirement housing, it would be as well for him or her to know the following things:

- **Retirement housing can be purchased,** rented or part rented/part bought, known as **shared ownership**.

- **There is usually a minimum age** at which your relative can live in retirement housing and this is often 60 or 55, occasionally 50. If the property is being purchased leasehold (see page 111), the age restriction will be set out in the lease. Some leases also include a restriction on the age of the person buying the lease, which means that a younger relative or friend cannot buy the lease in their own name. The management organisation or your relative's solicitor will be able to give more information.
- **Some housing has a scheme manager and an emergency alarm,** whereas others are designed for frailer older people and have 24-hour support and personal care services.

Jargon buster

Shared ownership Instead of paying the full price for a property, the purchaser pays a percentage (say, 50 per cent) of the equity and may pay rent on the remainder (depending on the specific terms of the shared ownership scheme). Shared ownership properties are usually restricted to people who do not have sufficient capital to buy on the open market

 For more information about buying and renting retirement housing, see pages 108-34, and for more information about leases, see pages 114-16.

- Retirement housing can be newly built, built some years ago, updated or part of an old house.
- There is retirement housing in **towns,** at the seaside and in rural areas. There are flats, some bungalows and a few houses.
- The average age of people moving into retirement housing is 72 and the majority of residents are in their eighties. However, there is often a range of ages and some residents may still be working.

❝Retirement housing can offer safety, security, peace of mind and plenty of companionship. ❞

WHY MOVE TO RETIREMENT HOUSING?

There are many reasons why people consider retirement housing, but most do so because they want:

- **The safety, security and peace of mind it offers.**
  - Flats often have door entry systems at the main door (and sometimes CCTV and intruder alarms) and locks on individual front doors, which also have their own letterboxes.
  - There is usually a scheme manager or housing officer who deals with major security issues.
  - Each flat has an emergency alarm which when activated contacts the scheme manager or a 24-hour call-monitoring centre who can contact relatives or the emergency services (see page 60).
  - The added reassurance that someone will keep an eye on their home if they are away for long periods.
- **There are no maintenance worries.**
  - Work that was your relative's responsibility as a householder is now the responsibility of the management organisation (see pages 127–8). This includes maintaining the external parts of the building, such as roof and drains; organising routine maintenance, such as the central heating, and arranging building insurance. The costs are then included in the service charge, which will be paid by your relative. Details about service charges are covered on pages 129–34.
- **Convenience.**
  - Retirement housing is usually situated in a convenient location near shops and buses.
  - It is often designed with no steps, wider than normal doorways and corridors, raised electrical sockets and easy-to-use taps.
- **Social opportunities and companionship.**
  - Communal areas such as the lounge provide opportunities for neighbours to meet and activities, such as coffee mornings and discussions, are often organised.
  - Your relative will not have to join in activities if he or she does not want to, but there is support available from both the scheme manager and other residents.

Questions to ask when choosing a retirement property

- What is the distance to the shops, banks, parks, doctor, pub and church?

- What is the distance to the bus stop and station? How frequently do the buses or trains run? Are any changes planned?

- Will it be convenient for friends and family to visit me?

- Will I like living exclusively with older people?

- Can I afford the accommodation, including the purchase price or rent and running costs, including service charges?

- Is there a lift should I need one?

- Are the doorways and corridors wide enough for people with walking frames and wheelchairs?

- Are doors and windows easy to operate and can light switches and electrical sockets be reached easily?

- Is the heating easy to control and economical to run?

- Is there room for my favourite furniture or will I have to buy smaller furniture?

- Is there adequate storage space?

- Are pets allowed?

- Is the security of both the main entrance (if there is one) and of individual front doors and windows adequate?

- Is there good insulation from the noise of the lift, rubbish chute, laundry, residents' lounge and next-door neighbours?

- What are the facilities for storing and charging electric scooters?

- What happens if I become frail and need more support than can be offered by a scheme manager and emergency alarm?

Possible downsides of retirement housing

- **Retirement housing is usually smaller** than a family home. So moving may mean getting rid of some furniture, books and ornaments.
- **The service charge** may also include charges for services that your relative may not use, such as a communal laundry.
- **Social activities** may not be of interest.
- **There will be no young people** and the neighbours are likely to be at home all day.
- **Rules about the use of the residents' lounge** and laundry may appear irksome if your relative has been used to doing things when he or she wants to do them.

THE COSTS

Retirement housing can be purchased (leasehold) from a developer, a private company or a housing association; rented from a housing association or the local council; rented privately or as shared ownership.

Purchase prices vary considerably depending on the area and the services provided. Service charges vary widely, too, ranging from a few pounds a week if there is no scheme manager to several hundred pounds a month, depending on whether meals and extra facilities are provided.

THE SCHEME MANAGER

In the last few years there have been many changes to the role of the scheme manager, who used to be known as the warden. The duties vary considerably according to the policies operated by the particular management organisation, however, there are usually two main parts of the job:

- **Getting to know the residents living in the scheme,** helping them to keep their independence by giving them information about local services that they could find useful and encouraging them to ask for extra support if the residents need it. When in the building, the scheme manager responds to the emergency alarm.
- **Managing the scheme;** for example, making sure the communal areas are cleaned, organising repairs and supervising the work of any contractors on the site (such as gardeners).

The scheme manager does not provide personal care, such as helping your relative get up in the mornings, nor do they do cleaning or shopping. The hours they keep at the scheme can vary, too:

- **A resident scheme manager** lives in a flat or bungalow on the site. In this case they usually work 35 hours a week and most are only available

For more information about buying and renting and all the associated costs, such as service charges and management organisation fees, see pages 107-34.

during working hours. If there is an emergency when the scheme manager is not on duty or not in the building, the resident can summon help through the emergency alarm.

- **A full-time non-resident manager** may have additional responsibilities in other schemes and in the local area, especially in housing association- or council-managed schemes.
- **Visiting or part-time manager,** who may spend only a short time – perhaps two hours, three times a week – in the scheme.

The scheme manager's salary and overheads, such as accommodation and office expenses, account for a large part of the service charge. Generally the fewer hours the scheme manager works, the lower the service charge.

❝ Wardens are also known as scheme managers. ❞

COMMUNAL FACILITIES

Retirement housing has a variety of facilities that can be used by all residents and sometimes by their families and/or friends or older people from the local area. These communal facilities may include lounge(s), often with a small kitchen attached, en-suite guest room, laundry, gardens and parking.

Points to consider about the communal facilities

For some people the communal facilities are very important, for others, less so. Depending on your relative's interests, he or she may want to find out how some of these facilities are organised and whether there are any 'rules' for residents to follow.

- Some retirement housing reserves the lounge for residents and their visitors, while in other cases people from the local community are encouraged to use it for events, meetings, classes and

Do your research

If your relative is interested in a particular scheme do encourage him or her to ask the scheme manager, housing officer or management organisation about:

- The scheme manager's duties.
- Their hours of work.
- What happens if your relative needs emergency help when the scheme manager is off duty?
- Whether any changes are planned or being considered for the way in which the service is delivered.
- The amount of the service charge and, if appropriate, whether your relative can get any financial help towards the charges (see pages 111-15).

advice surgeries. Who decides who can use the lounge? Could your relative hire the lounge for, say, a birthday party or family event?

- **The guest room** is an en-suite bedroom, usually with a shower, which residents can book for their guests. There is usually a small charge and sometimes a maximum number of nights for which it can be booked. How is it booked? Is it ever used for temporary staff and what happens to the money charged? Have the 'rules' been agreed by all the residents or by the residents' association on behalf of all the residents?
- **The washers and dryers in the laundry should be easy to use.** Are there any outside drying areas? Will your relative have to bend down to put the clothes in? They may be coin or token operated or paid for through the service charge. During what hours can the laundry be used? Can the laundry be used by carers or relatives?
- **The arrangements for disposing of rubbish and recycling will vary.** If your relative is likely to have difficulty carrying his or her rubbish to the chute or refuse area, your relative may want to talk to the scheme manager or housing officer to see what alternative arrangements can be made.
- **If your relative has a car or expects visitors who will need parking,** the parking facilities may need checking.
- **Communal gardens** are usually maintained by the management organisation; individual gardens will be identified in your relative's lease or tenancy agreement. Your relative may want to know about the arrangements for upkeep of the garden, whether he or she can do some gardening and whether there are any restrictions on its use.

RESIDENTS' ASSOCIATION

All good management organisations should have policies that encourage the formation of residents' associations. An active residents' association can represent residents' interests in discussions with the management organisation and help organise social activities. Under the Association of Retirement Housing

Communal areas in Scotland

In Scotland, property is purchased freehold. The Deed of Conditions, which forms part of the title deeds, should spell out the rules for the common areas of the retirement housing. If the title deeds do not contain the information, your relative should consult the Tenement Management Scheme (TMS). This was introduced in 2004 to make it easier for owners to carry out repairs and maintenance to the common areas of their property.

For more details visit: http://scotland.shelter.org.uk.

Managers (ARHM) Code of Practice (England only), management organisations should recognise any residents' association that has a proper constitution, elected officers and represents the majority of properties on site. Membership of a residents' association is not compulsory – your relative does not have to join.

CHARITIES AND SPECIALIST HOUSING

There are some specialist charities and housing associations that provide retirement housing to rent.

Abbeyfield Societies

There are over 700 Abbeyfield houses situated throughout the UK, which are run by a federation of independent, local and mainly volunteer-run charities. Abbeyfield houses provide supported sheltered housing to rent for people over 55 who are reasonably fit but no longer wish to live on their own. Most Abbeyfield Societies run either one or several houses in the same area, each providing a home for around 8–12 older people. A typical Abbeyfield house provides:

- **A paid house manager** who is responsible for ensuring that the house runs smoothly, looks after the meals and ensures the communal areas are cleaned.

- **Private bed-sitting rooms,** usually with en-suite facilities, which residents can furnish themselves.
- **Two meals a day.**
- **A shared dining room** and often a shared sitting room and garden.
- **An emergency call system,** which provides 24-hour cover.
- **Support and fellowship** from a network of local volunteers.

Most Abbeyfield residents have tenancy agreements but a few have licences (see page 145). Rents and admission criteria vary from house to house, so your relative should inquire at the particular house where he or she is hoping to become a resident. While visiting, it is a good idea to check what would happen if your relative needed help with personal care in the future.

Abbeyfield Societies also run care homes in England, Wales and Scotland. These have to be registered with the social care registration authority and residents needing financial help have to be assessed by their local council.

Almshouses

Almshouses provide rented housing, often adapted and designed for older people. Each almshouse charity is independent and run by volunteer trustees. There are nearly 2,000 separate almshouse charities throughout England and Wales,

 To find details of specific local Abbeyfield Societies together with answers to FAQs, go to www.abbeyfield.com.

providing affordable homes to around 36,000 people. The almshouse movement is over 1,000 years old and some of the early dwellings are still in use today. They vary considerably in size from just two units of accommodation to 1,800 units.

- **Historically, almshouse charities included age, gender, geographic or occupational requirements** in their governing documents, but now this has usually been simplified to 'persons in need', which is often interpreted as someone in receipt of a means-tested benefit such as Pension Credit, from a specific geographical area.
- **A resident occupies an almshouse under a very simple form of licence** called a 'letter of appointment', which does not constitute a tenancy, so there is no security of tenure.

Specialist housing

There is a limited amount of specialist retirement housing for people with:

- Specific cultural, ethnic or religious needs, such as Jewish and Asian people.
- Poor mobility, such as wheelchair users and blind people, although most newly built retirement housing is designed to meet the needs of people with poor mobility.

- Specific medical conditions, such as dementia.
- Specific occupational backgrounds, such as teachers and people from the Armed Services.

To live in a specific area, your relative may need to consider almshouses or Abbeyfield houses.

Park homes

Park homes are single-storey residential mobile homes, some resembling bungalows and others like caravans. There are about 250,000 people living in park homes on more than 1,700 sites in England and Wales. According to government statistics, almost half park home households in the UK are retired people. Points to be aware of include:

- **Park homes can be bought relatively cheaply,** often for around half the cost of an equivalent sized 'bricks and mortar' property. If your relative buys a park home, he or she will also have to pay the site owner a rent for the pitch and for maintenance of communal areas. Site rental fees vary, depending on the size and position of the site.
- **All privately owned sites must be licensed by the local council** and the site licence must, by law, be displayed where residents can see it.

To find out more about almshouses, visit www.HousingCare.org/housing/search.aspx and then select 'Almshouse Charity' in the 'Provider' window. Your relative should then contact the specific almshouse charity for information on their criteria for admission, rents and vacancies.

- **Your relative should have a written agreement** with the site owner. This is a legal requirement.
- **The site owner should be a member of** the British Holiday and Home Parks Association (BHHPA). Generally this means that the site is more likely to be well maintained and your relative is more likely to receive a good standard of service.
- **The site rental costs** and other services the site owner provides and the obligation of the park home owner to pay and how often the charges are reviewed.
- **The responsibilities of the site owner** and the park home owner, such as the pitch fees.
- **The site should be well maintained.**
- **What restrictions and costs apply** when selling a park home. The site owner must approve the potential purchaser but cannot legally withhold

approval unreasonably. The site owner can claim commission to a legal maximum of 10 per cent of the sale price of the park home.

If your relative is interested in buying a park home, he or she is advised to get a copy of 'Mobile homes – a guide for residents and site owners', which describes the responsibilities of both the resident and site owner and includes a sample written agreement (see below).

FINDING RETIREMENT HOUSING

Your relative's local council will have details of retirement housing in his or her area (to find your local council, see box at foot of page 33). In addition, Elderly Accommodation Counsel (EAC) (see bow below), has a database with details of all the housing for older people in the UK.

Elderly Accommodation Counsel (EAC)

EAC is a small national charity that offers free information and advice to older people and their families on all forms of accommodation and services for older people. The EAC's national database of housing for older people contains information about 26,000 retirement housing schemes and 14,000 care homes throughout the UK. The details are available to view and download on www.HousingCare.org. The advice line is on 020 7820 1343.

 For a copy of the guide 'Mobile homes' go to www.communities.gov.uk/publications/ housing/ mobilehomes. The content also applies to Scotland. A list of UK mobile home sites can be found on www.ukparks.com. The website for BHHPA is www.bhhpa.org.uk.

Extra care housing

Extra care housing is retirement housing with personal care, meals and 24-hour support available for those that need it. It is sometimes called very sheltered housing, close care, assisted living or a retirement village. People living in extra care housing have the security and privacy of their own home and the legal right to occupy the property.

New forms of extra care housing have been developed in recent years with government support. In England, the Government, through the Department of Health, has invested significant sums of money in developing extra care housing as part of their reconfiguring of services for older people.

Extra care housing caters for older people who are becoming frailer and less able to do things for themselves. Most older people want to live independently in their own homes for as long as possible, so extra care housing is a popular choice for older people and their relatives. It can often enable couples who have different needs to stay together and can sometimes offer an alternative to a care home.

CHOOSING EXTRA CARE HOUSING

There is no standard type of extra care housing. It comes in many forms,

including blocks of flats, bungalow estates and retirement villages, and has a variety of different services, including an emergency alarm service, restaurants/ dining rooms, domestic help and hairdressing salons. There is a limited (although increasing) amount of extra care housing in most areas and the majority of providers set criteria that prospective residents have to meet.

Extra care housing providers use different terms to describe the services and facilities they offer. The main terms that are used are:

Very sheltered housing and assisted living

These are terms used by some providers to describe housing that provides meals, domestic assistance and 24-hour housekeeping staff cover to enable older people to remain in their own home for as long as possible. It also describes a US

For more information about extra care housing in all its wide variety, go to the EAC website at www.HousingCare.org.

model of hotel-style care facilities for older people who no longer live in their own home, but do not need medical supervision or nursing care.

Retirement villages

Retirement villages offer a variety of types of accommodation specifically for older people. They have many community facilities and are usually in an attractive rural setting. A typical retirement village will have over 100 dwellings of different types, such as one-, two- and three-bedroom flats and bungalows, to buy, rent (usually at market rents), or shared ownership. They will also have a restaurant, clubroom, library, shop, laundry, cleaning services, leisure facilities and perhaps a medical centre, carers and a minibus; some will have a care centre that provides 24-hour nursing care. Most retirement villages have a range of activities where residents who like to socialise can join with like-minded people. They are common in the US and Australia but are relatively new in this country.

Close care

This type of extra care housing offers a small group, often 6–20, of self-contained flats or bungalows built on the same site as a care home. Residents usually have some services, such as an emergency alarm and use of a handyperson, included in their service charge and they can buy other services such as personal care, laundry and meals from the care home. Residents can often choose whether to go to the restaurant for meals or have the meals delivered to their own home.

Choosing an appropriate form of housing

As different housing providers use different terms to describe their retirement housing and extra care housing, choosing a service to meet your relative's needs and wishes can be difficult. Furthermore, because of the variety, it is important that you and your relative are sure the service will meet your relative's needs. You should both ask as many questions as you need to about the services, facilities and how they are paid for (see page 97). In particular, your relative should find out:

- What services are provided.
- Which services are included in the service charge and which are charged as extras.
- Whether your relative is eligible for any financial help. The scheme manager, housing officer or local advice agency, such as Citizens Advice or Age Concern, may be able to help.

 To find details of your relative's local CAB, go to www.adviceguide.org.uk. For details of local Age Concerns, go to www.ageconcern.org.uk (England), www.accymru.org.uk (Wales), www.ageconcernscotland.org.uk (Scotland) or www.ageconcernni.org (Northern Ireland).

Seek independent professional advice before signing any lease or tenancy agreement. For more information, go to www.unbiased.co.uk, the FSA website that helps you find a local independent financial adviser, or Solicitors for the Elderly at www.solicitorsfortheelderly.com.

EXTRA CARE HOUSING MANAGEMENT

Extra care housing can be rented through a housing association or the local council, purchased (leasehold) in a development managed either by a commercial company or a not-for-profit organisation, or as shared ownership. Much of the newly built extra care housing is **mixed tenure**. There is usually a scheme manager or housekeeper who manages the building and on-site staff and liaises with other organisations that provide care, support and lifestyle services.

FINDING EXTRA CARE HOUSING

Your relative's local council will have details of extra care housing in his or her area or use the EAC website (see below).

Jargon buster

Mixed tenure Retirement housing that has some properties to buy (leasehold), some to rent and some identified for shared ownership. These developments are mainly owned and managed by housing associations

❝There are many ways to own or rent extra care housing, which is provided by a range of not-for-profit and commercial suppliers. ❞

 To find your relative's local council visit www.direct.gov.uk. Visit www.HousingCare.org or ring EAC Advice Line on 020 7820 1343.

Buy or rent?

A growing number of older people are questioning the need to own their own home. For some, the attraction of releasing equity from their bricks and mortar is appealing; others value the security that owning gives or the services provided by social housing landlords. Retirement housing can be purchased or rented to meet individual needs and wishes.

Buying retirement housing

Most retirement housing is **leasehold** rather than **freehold** and purchased at full price on the open market. But if your relative is not able to raise the purchase price or has limited income, he or she may like to explore some of the options that are described in this section.

EARLY STAGES

The process of buying retirement housing is much the same as buying other leasehold property, but there are two clauses in retirement housing leases (Deed of Condition in Scotland) that your relative will need to be aware of at an early stage in the buying process.

Age restriction

The lease will almost always specify a minimum age at which your relative will be able to live in retirement housing. There is no consistent age, but it is usually 60 or 55, occasionally 50. This restriction may sometimes also apply to the person who is buying the lease on behalf of an older person. This age restriction may also mean that your relative would not be able to have a live-in carer (under the minimum age) if that became necessary. So if you are in this position it is worth checking with the salesperson or management organisation before proceeding.

Management organisation approval

Many retirement housing leases require the management organisation to approve the potential buyer after he or she has made an offer and before the sale proceeds. The prospective buyer is often required to be in reasonable health and be able to lead an independent life. To ensure that this is so, most management organisations will want a member of their staff (often the scheme manager) to interview the prospective buyer and some will ask for a GP's letter for which your relative may have to pay.

The salesperson

If your relative is interested in buying a new retirement property, he or she will probably initially visit the show flat and deal with the salesperson. The salesperson's job is to make the process of buying as easy as possible. He or she can often help with finding an estate agent to sell your relative's current home

 For more information about purchasing a leasehold property, see the *Which? Essential Guide: Buy, Sell and Move House*.

or finding a removal company. The salesperson can also explain any special services the developer may be offering, such as part-exchange deals.

Part exchange

Some developers and selling agents offer deals, especially on new retirement property, where they buy your relative's home in part exchange for payment for their new flat. These can be very useful in helping to ensure a quick and easy move, but they may offer less than the full market price for your relative's current home. Do encourage your relative to get an open market valuation through two or three estate agents for his or her current property before deciding whether or not to pursue the offer of part exchange.

Other services

Some developers and selling agents offer a range of other services, including bridging finance, managing every aspect of the move, interior design and

maintenance services. Again, depending on your relative's circumstances it may be worth costing these services on the open market. More information about any current deals can be obtained from the salesperson or the developer.

GETTING A MORTGAGE

Some banks and building societies may offer mortgages to help with the purchase of retirement housing.

Interest-only mortgage

An interest-only mortgage allows homeowners to borrow a cash lump sum via a mortgage secured on their property. As long as interest payments are made monthly, the borrowed amount never increases. The original loan is only repaid when the term of the mortgage ends or the property is sold. Usually, borrowers are encouraged to maintain a separate repayment vehicle, such as an endowment or ISAs, so the original loan can be repaid at the end of the term.

Pros and cons of an interest-only mortgage	
Pros	Cons
• Because only the interest is being repaid and not the capital, monthly payments are lower than for a repayment mortgage (see page 110).	• The original amount borrowed never reduces and there is no guarantee that the endowment or ISAs will produce enough money to repay the debt at the end of the term. • If the interest rate is not fixed for the full term and interest rates rise, borrowers who enter retirement and rely on a fixed pension may struggle to meet the additional cost of increased monthly repayments.

Repayment mortgage

This form of mortgage allows homeowners to borrow a cash lump sum via a mortgage secured on their property. Each month a proportion of the monthly repayment is used to not only repay the interest but to also reduce some of the capital that was originally borrowed. As long as the monthly payments continue to be paid for the term of the mortgage, when it is complete there will no longer be a debt.

❝ Those with a good life expectancy are better off with a repayment mortgage. An interest-only loan might suit people in poor health. ❞

Points to consider when getting a mortgage

- If your relative needs a mortgage, he or she will still have to make similar decisions as a younger person might have to make in choosing a mortgage and should contact an independent financial adviser who specialises in mortgages.

  If your relative can afford it and has a good life expectancy, then it is generally better to choose a repayment mortgage. But if your relative is in poor health and has a shortened life expectancy, then an interest-only mortgage might be preferable. As a rule, it is thought that no more than 20 per cent of anyone's retirement income should be required for mortgage repayment.
- Not all banks or building societies will offer mortgages on retirement property.

Pros and cons of a repayment mortgage

Pros	Cons
• There is no need to maintain a separate investment vehicle to clear the original balance at the end of the mortgage term, as each month the amount owed reduces until the amount outstanding is zero.	• In the first few years, the monthly repayments are mainly used to repay the interest, so the amount borrowed will not be greatly reduced. • If the interest rate is not fixed for the full term of the mortgage, and interest rates rise, borrowers who enter retirement and rely on a fixed pension may struggle to meet the additional cost of increased monthly repayments.

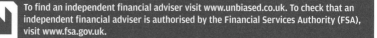 To find an independent financial adviser visit www.unbiased.co.uk. To check that an independent financial adviser is authorised by the Financial Services Authority (FSA), visit www.fsa.gov.uk.

Traditional mortgage lenders tend to restrict eligibility for their mortgages as clients get older. This can vary from lender to lender and can be as low as 65 years of age or as high as 85 years of age. Very few lenders will allow an open-ended term, although this would be a highly recommended feature if available.

An affordability assessment allows the lender to assess each borrower's ability to afford the monthly repayments. It is crucial that every borrower considers the impact any future increases in the monthly repayments may have on his or her disposable income. A long-term fixed interest rate can help reduce the risk associated with future rate changes. For example, if your relative is aged 60 years, he or she may find lenders prepared to offer a 25-year term whereas, at the age of 70, this might be reduced to ten years.

- **The amount that can be borrowed** will be subject to the value of the property your relative is buying, his or her income and the conditions imposed by the lender. The lower the amount your relative needs to borrow compared to the value of the property, the more likely lenders will be to consider a mortgage.

LEASEHOLD AND SHARED-OWNERSHIP SCHEMES

If your relative has a limited income and insufficient capital to buy retirement housing on the open market, he or she may be interested in finding out about leasehold schemes for the elderly (LSE) and shared-ownership schemes for the elderly (SOSE). Both these schemes are run by a small number of housing associations scattered around the country who have properties that were built with government grants. No new properties are being built but re-sales are sometimes available.

Leasehold schemes for the elderly (LSE)

When LSE properties are put on the market they are valued by the housing association and then the lease is sold at a percentage of the market value (say, 70 per cent) with the freehold and remaining percentage of the equity being retained by the housing association. When your relative sells, he or she would receive the same percentage of the market value, the rest is retained by the housing association.

In addition to the capital paid, your relative would usually pay the full service charge and possibly ground rent. If your relative receives Housing Benefit, financial help may be available with the rent and service charge and the **housing related support charge** (see page 126).

Jargon buster

Housing related support charge The charge for services including the emergency alarm and/or the scheme manager. These services include emergency help, emotional advice and support and guidance on benefits

111

Shared-ownership schemes for the elderly (SOSE)

In SOSE schemes, your relative buys up to 75 per cent of the value of the property and pays rent on all but the final 25 per cent (which usually cannot be purchased and is rent free).

New shared-ownership schemes

Some housing associations are now building extra care housing in mixed tenure schemes that include shared-ownership properties. In these schemes your relative would buy 25 per cent, 50 per cent or 75 per cent of the equity in the property and pay rent on all but the final 25 per cent (which usually cannot be purchased and is rent free).

If your relative has a low income and savings of less than £16,000, he or she may be eligible for housing benefit to help with the rent.

Points to consider when thinking about an LSE or SOSE

- The length of the lease remaining.
- Whether the purchase has to be a cash purchase because, in a very few cases, the lease precludes getting a mortgage.
- Whether any rent has to be paid on the non-owned equity of an SOSE.
- Whether there will be additional charges, such as service charge and/or

ground rent. Some properties built in the late 1980s or early 1990s may be approaching a ground rent review (see page 134).

- **What the arrangements will be for selling the property** and whether the housing association will make any deductions from the sale price.
- **If the lease states that the housing association will find a buyer,** check in what circumstances your relative (or his or her estate) can advertise the property on the open market. The housing association will usually reserve the right to approve any prospective buyer to ensure he or she is sufficiently independent and because most shared-ownership schemes are for older people who cannot afford the full market price of retirement housing.

Acquiring a shared-ownership property

If your relative is interested in shared ownership, contact www.HousingCare.org, the website for Elderly Accommodation Counsel (EAC) (see box on page 103) or use their advice line for details of housing associations that are offering these schemes. Then contact the housing association concerned who will guide your relative through their procedures. Your relative may be required to provide details of his or her finances to demonstrate eligibility.

 To contact EAC, go to www.HousingCare.org. For more information about service charges and ground rents including ground rent reviews, go to page 137.

Selling a shared-ownership property

When selling, the property may have to be sold to someone nominated by the housing association to ensure the prospective buyer is eligible (for example, has limited means) and there may be deductions from the proceeds of the sale, such as for a contribution to the reserve fund (see page 130) or a charge to the housing association.

LIFETIME LEASE

A lifetime lease is sometimes called a life interest plan and is an arrangement where a commercial company buys a property and sells your relative the right to live in that property for the rest of his or her life or, in the case of a couple, for both their lives. A lifetime lease is only available to people aged 60 and over and when the leaseholder(s) dies, the property reverts to the commercial company.

The cost of a lifetime lease is based on a sliding scale that relates to your relative's age, gender and marital status. It is typically 30–50 per cent of the cost of an outright purchase.

❝ With a lifetime lease the property reverts to the lender after death. ❞

Pros and cons of a lifetime lease

Pros
- If your relative is currently a homeowner, he or she may be able to release capital by moving to a property with a lifetime lease. This capital could be used to supplement your relative's pension, improve his or her standard of living or, perhaps, help family.
- Your relative may be able to move to an area or a type of property they otherwise may not be able to afford. This may mean your relative can move closer to his or her family.
- A property held through a lifetime lease will not form part of your relative's estate for inheritance tax purposes.

Cons
- Releasing capital may affect any means-tested benefits to which your relative is entitled because he or she will have a capital sum of over £6,000 and for every £500 over the £6,000 threshold, £1 is added to other income.
- If your relative is not happy in the lifetime lease property or he or she needs to move again, your relative will not recoup the bulk of the original capital. This may limit future choices.
- Your relative will not be able to use an equity release plan (see page 79) to raise income or capital from the property, should he or she need to in the future.

For more information about inheritance tax, see the *Which? Essential Guide* to *Giving and Inheriting*.

It is strongly recommended that your relative seeks advice from an IFA or solicitor who is independent of the company selling the lifetime lease.

If your relative decides to move out, he or she would only get back a small proportion (around 10 per cent maximum) of the amount originally paid. As well as the initial payment, a lifetime leaseholder is responsible for paying council tax, utility bills and service charges.

> ❝ Sale-and-rent-back schemes are proving popular but do encourage your relative to explore all the implications. ❞

SALE-AND-RENT-BACK SCHEMES

Sale-and-rent-back are schemes where your relative would sell his or her property to a company for less than its market value, typically 70–80 per cent, and then rent it back from the purchasing company at a normal market rent. The fees and costs involved would probably have to be paid by your relative.

Your relative would then be able to use the cash proceeds to pay off the mortgage (or any other debts) or use the money in some other way while remaining in the property. It is possible sometimes to buy the property back from the company at the market rate in the future if your relative can afford it.

Sale-and-rent-back schemes are being widely advertised, however concerns have been expressed about the fact that:

- **Scheme providers** are not registered with the FSA and have been targeting vulnerable people.
- **Providers have not been offering** a secure tenancy to provide the security of being able to remain in the property over the long term.
- **There are no guarantees of future rent levels** and it has been reported that some homeowners who are desperate for cash have fallen victim to unregulated firms buying their property and renting it back to them with rent increases they cannot afford.
- **There is a danger that if the new landlord doesn't keep up with any mortgage commitments** the property could be repossessed.

In 2008, the National Association Sale and Rent Back (NASARB) proposed a voluntary Code of Practice for the sector, but at the time of writing, the details have not been announced.

 The FSA website is www.fsa.gov.uk or contact the FSA via their consumer helpline on 0845 606 1234.

Which? advises readers to avoid these schemes until they are regulated. But if your relative chooses to pursue a sale-and-rent-back scheme, it is essential to look at the terms of any rental agreements and check that they contain guarantees that your relative can remain in their home for as long as he or she wishes to and for as long as your relative continues to pay the rent.

- That the provisions in the agreement are reasonable, for example, are the terms flexible if your relative is late in paying the rent?
- Is the landlord a genuine and credible company?
- Whether, after your relative has signed the agreement, the landlord is able to terminate the tenancy if he or she chooses.
- Whether your relative knows who is responsible for such things as maintaining the building and paying the utility bills.

Important checks

If your relative is interested in looking at a sale-or-rent-back scheme, it is imperative that he or she bears in mind the following points:

- Companies offering a lease for life must be authorised by the FSA. Ask the company for their FSA registration number and check on the FSA website or helpline (see box opposite below).
- Whether the rent is likely to increase and how often and by how much.
- Whether your relative will be able to afford to rent back the property for as long as he or she plans to stay in it.

If your relative comes across any unusual arrangements for financing the purchase of retirement housing, such as a request for an interest-free loan in exchange for a tenancy for life, it is imperative he or she seeks specialist advice (see box, opposite top) before proceeding.

❝ It is vital to consider the terms of the agreement such as for late payment or tenancy security in sale or rent-back schemes. ❞

For more detailed information about the legal aspects of leasing retirement housing, see pages 134-48.

Selling your relative's home

Selling a property that may well have been the family home for many years can be a very emotional and stressful experience for all involved; particularly if the older person is moving to an environment that is unfamiliar to him or her. But if all other options have been considered, then dealing with the sale as sensitively as possible is important.

If your relative is moving into rented accommodation or a care home, it may be better for your relative to delay giving up his or her current home for a short period, in case a wrong decision has been made.

> **"** Wait for a short period to ensure your relative is happy with his or her new accommodation before selling the old property. **"**

GOOD SELLING PRACTICE

While this is not the book to go into selling a property in depth, here are a few tips to help the sale go as smoothly as possible.

- Choosing the right estate agent to market the property is important. Pick up a local property paper and look at who is successfully selling similar properties and then negotiate with them their charges for selling your relative's home. Most estate agents belong to the National Association of Estate Agents (NAEA), which has a Code of Practice for its members.
- Check your relative orders a Home Information Pack (HIP), which is now a requirement by law for vendors in England and Wales.
- Ensure your relative is selling at the right price. It is advisable to obtain

The Community Legal Services produces a useful fact sheet called 'Buying and selling a property - your legal rights', which can be downloaded from www.clsdirect.org.uk. See also the NAEA website: www.naea.co.uk. For more information on selling property, see the *Which? Essential Guide: Buy, Sell and Move House.*

valuations from two or more estate agents as well as looking in the local paper to see what similar properties are selling for.

- **Your relative's property may need some essential repairs** or tidying up to make it as attractive as possible to potential buyers. Your estate agent should be able to advise you as to what work would be economically sensible to carry out to achieve a sale.
- **Get the legalities of selling a property right** and to do this your relative may already have a family solicitor who can handle the legal side of things. Before you instruct him or her, ask about fees. Some solicitors will deal with property conveyancing for fixed fees.

BRIDGING FINANCE

If your relative is relying on the proceeds of the sale of his or her current property to purchase retirement housing but is unable to wait for the sale to complete, there are schemes available to assist in managing the whole process and provide bridging finance.

Normally these schemes would offer a managed sale service for a fee of around 2.5 per cent, which would cover estate agent and standard legal fees. However, they can also offer bridging finance to help purchase a new property or assist with the cost of care home fees while the property is being sold and other services, which must be negotiated separately, like garden maintenance, house clearance, removals and Home Information Packs.

This sort of service can be particularly useful if you are living a distance away from your relative's property and find it difficult to visit it regularly to carry out routine maintenance like cutting the grass or cleaning.

Details of such schemes should be available from a financial adviser who has the qualification CF8, which combines financial advice with the complexities of the care system.

DISPOSAL OF POSSESSIONS

The other issue to consider is the sensitive way you may need to dispose of some of the contents of your relative's former home, much of which might be cherished possessions, but just cannot be accommodated in the retirement housing your relative is moving to. If possible, you should involve your relative in this process and in deciding what to do with various items.

It may be necessary to employ a house clearance company or perhaps a local charity will collect and accept some of the contents. It might be quite hard to dispose of old family photographs or your relative's private letters, so perhaps these could be boxed and taken with them. Supplies of old drugs should be disposed of carefully, ideally returning them to your relative's GP or local pharmacy.

❝ If possible, involve your relative in the sensitive disposal of his or her possessions. ❞

Privately rented housing

Over 70 per cent of households in the UK are now owner occupied, but a growing number of older people are choosing to rent rather than buy in retirement. Industry sources estimate that about 60 per cent of older people looking to rent retirement housing are homeowners.

Privately rented retirement housing is retirement housing rented at market rents from a private company or individual, rather than from the council or a housing association. A privately rented flat is likely to be either in a block where most of the other flats are owned by leaseholders on long leases or in a block where all the properties are let at market rents. There is a small but growing demand for privately rented retirement housing from people who want to release equity from their homes (see page 79).

SHORT OR LONG LET?

If your relative is thinking about privately rented retirement housing, the most important thing he or she needs to consider is whether to rent for a short period or for long-term security. This will determine the sort of tenancy your relative should look for. If he or she wants a short let (six months), perhaps to check out an area or to

sample what it's like to live in retirement housing, an assured shorthold tenancy may suit his or her needs. If, however, your relative is looking for long-term security, he or she should look for an assured tenancy.

RENT

The ways in which rent is charged depends on the type of tenancy your relative takes out:

- **If the tenancy is for a fixed period,** such as for an assured shorthold tenancy for six months, the rent will remain the same for that period.
- **If it is for longer or is regularly reviewed by the landlord,** there will normally be a rent review clause in the tenancy agreement. This will usually allow the rent to increase by a specific amount, such as in accordance with the retail price index (RPI) on the anniversary of the date the tenancy began.

 See pages 142–5 for further information about tenancies and tenancy agreements.

It is always a good idea to try to negotiate the rent in privately rented property. Rents in private rented retirement housing are market rents and vary widely and usually include the service charge and ground rent. Rents are usually paid each calendar month by direct debit or standing order.

FINDING PRIVATELY RENTED RETIREMENT HOUSING

The first thing to do is to contact the local letting agents in the area in which your relative wants to live – the local paper online is often a useful source of information. The Association of Registered Letting Agents (ARLA) requires their members to work according to a Code of Practice, which provides a framework of ethical and professional standards higher than that demanded in law. You can also sound out the following organisations to see if they know of any local retirement housing with privately rented vacancies:

- **The scheme manager of leasehold retirement housing** in the area in which your relative is interested.
- **The website for EAC** (see box, bottom).
- **Specialists** in privately rented retirement housing (see also below).
- **The local council's** housing advice service.

The pros and cons of privately rented retirement housing

Pros	Cons
• If your relative has sold his or her property, capital can be released and used to supplement his or her pension, improve your relative's standard of living or, perhaps, help family.	• Your relative no longer owns his or her home and may therefore lose out if property prices rise.
• Your relative can reduce any debts, such as a mortgage.	• If your relative sells a property, he or she may lose entitlement to means-tested benefits such as Pension Credit (see page 30).
• The monthly rental usually includes service charges and ground rent, which makes financial planning easier. Likewise, the rent rises are likely be in line with the RPI, perhaps capped at a specific level per year.	• Using capital to pay rent may mean your relative has less to leave as legacies.

 Useful websites for finding privately rented retirement housing are: www.arla.co.uk (for ARLA's Code of Practice); www.HousingCare.org (the website for EAC), and www.girlings.co.uk, who specialise in privately rented retirement housing.

Renting social housing

Local councils and housing associations usually offer their housing to people in the greatest housing need and at rents that are affordable – perhaps with the help of Housing Benefit. They set criteria describing who qualifies for their housing and who has the highest priority. In most areas they receive applications from more people than they can assist.

SOCIAL HOUSING

When housing is rented through the council or housing associations, it is often known as social housing.

Renting through the council

Until recently, local councils were the main providers of rented retirement housing but this has now changed. Recent housing legislation, the age and condition of council properties and the lack of new building by councils mean that they now manage a decreasing amount of retirement housing. Many councils, for example, have transferred their properties to housing associations and others have established separate organisations to manage their housing, such as the **Arms Length Management Organisations** (ALMOs). This means that housing associations are now the main providers of rented retirement housing.

Council housing authorities are required by law (Housing Act 1996, as amended by the Homelessness Act 2002) to have an allocation policy (sometimes called an allocation scheme), which determines the priorities and sets out the allocation procedures for housing in their area. This policy is set by local councillors and has to meet local needs and take account of likely demand. A summary of this is available, free of charge, from the local council. Your relative can also get a copy of the full policy, but there is likely to be a charge for this.

Housing associations

Housing associations are non-profit-making organisations that provide and manage housing for people who cannot afford to buy on the open market. Housing associations may be charities or **registered industrial and provident societies** or both and are sometimes

 To find out more about Arms Length Management Organisations (ALMOs), go to www.communities.gov.uk/armslengthmanagement.

120

Social housing versus privately rented housing

This table highlights the differences between the three forms of rented retirement housing. Similarities between the three forms include a scheme manager, who can either be resident, non-resident, full time, part time or visiting; emergency cover, so that an alarm system is usually available; and communal facilities, which are usually a lounge and may also have a laundry. Personal care is not usually available, although services can be provided through the local council following a needs assessment (see pages 38–48). Residents can also arrange and pay for their own help.

Feature	Council	Housing association	Private
Mainly for people who:	• Have a housing need, need the support of retirement housing and can live independently with additional care services if necessary	• Similar to council	• Are not eligible for social housing or who choose not to apply or who want to rent for a short period
Accommodation	• Mostly one bedroom and bedsits • Let unfurnished • Own front door • Likely to be older than housing associations	• Mostly one-bedroom flats, some bedsits • Let unfurnished • Own front door • Likely to be newer properties than council	• Mostly one-bedroom flats • Mostly let unfurnished • Own front door • Likely to be more modern than social housing
Rent and support charges	• Affordable rents, which used to be lower than housing associations, but are now similar and will be the same by 2012 • Vary widely throughout the country • Rent charge usually includes service charge with an additional housing support charge	• Affordable rents, which used to be higher than councils but now similar and will be the same by 2012 • Vary widely throughout the country • Rent and service charges are usually included, but set out separately on the annual rent review notice • There is an additional housing support charge (see page 126)	• Market rent, which usually includes service charge and ground rent • Rent is usually increased annually by the RPI, sometimes with a ceiling, say, up to a maximum of 6%
Tenure	• May be an introductory tenancy for the first year then a secure tenancy (see page 143)	• May be an assured shorthold tenancy for the first 12 months then an assured tenancy if started after 15 January 1989 (see page 145)	• May be an assured tenancy or assured shorthold tenancy (see page 145)

known as Registered Social Landlords (RSLs). They are mainly funded by the Housing Corporation (England), Welsh Assembly Housing Directorate, Communities Scotland or Northern Ireland Housing Executive.

THE APPLICATION PROCESS

If your relative thinks he or she is eligible for council or housing association retirement housing, is not at present a council or housing association tenant and would like to apply, then your relative should contact the local council and tell them he or she wants to apply for retirement housing. This can be done in person, over the telephone or in writing.

Application procedures vary from area to area, but all councils have to follow certain rules and most will have a leaflet explaining how their system works. All councils are required by law to provide free information on:

- How to make an application.
- Who is eligible to be considered for housing.
- How the priorities between applicants are decided (see pages 124–5).
- The procedures that will be followed when the council considers your relative's application.
- What happens when a suitable property becomes available.

Councils also have a responsibility to help applicants who find it difficult to apply, perhaps because they are elderly or because English is not their first language. Some councils, for instance, will interview all applicants for retirement housing.

Applying for social housing

Step 1 Fill in the application form. The council's housing department sends your relative an application form and may give him or her an appointment to see a housing officer. Each council has its own application form but most application forms will ask for:

- The name, age and gender of everyone in your relative's household.
- Your relative's income and that of anyone else in the household.

 More information about what to expect from a housing association is available from the Housing Corporation booklet, 'A Charter for housing association applicants and residents' (April 2007) available on www.housingcorp.gov.uk.

- **Your relative's current address** and the facilities he or she has, and any previous addresses (usually for the past five years).
- **Whether your relative** (if not local) has any connections with the area.
- **Your relative's reason for wanting to move,** such as medical reasons or to be near his or her family who can give support.
- **The type of accommodation needed,** including the number of bedrooms, location and any facilities. The more flexible your relative can be about the location, the more chance he or she then has of being allocated a property.
- **Whether your relative has any special requirements,** such as the need for wheelchair access.

The council may, with your relative's agreement, seek additional information perhaps from his or her GP, if they decide it is necessary from what your relative has told them.

It is important that the application form is completed in full because this will help the council assess your relative's priority for housing. For example, if there are any factors that make your relative's need urgent (such as soon to become homeless or sharing facilities with another family), do make sure the council knows as soon as possible.

Step 2 The council considers your relative's application for housing. Once they have decided whether your relative is eligible, they will write confirming that his or her name is on the housing register, giving a registration number and the level of priority given to their application. If your relative disagrees with a housing decision and wishes to appeal, he or she should get an appeal form from the council offices, complete it and send it to the address on the form (see also pages 203–4).

It is important to remember that being eligible for an allocation does not necessarily mean that your relative will be offered a property as in some areas the demand for properties far outweighs the number that are available.

The council will write to your relative (usually annually) to ask if his or her circumstances have changed.

Step 3 Being on the waiting list. Once your relative's name is on the waiting list he or she may have to wait some time for housing unless the council has decided there is an urgent need. The length of wait depends on the number of people on the housing register who want retirement housing, the priority given to your relative's application, the number of properties that become vacant and how specific are your relative's needs.

 To find your relative's local council, look in the phone book or visit www.direct.gov.uk.

If your relative wants to move from a family home to a retirement flat, suggest he or she asks the council if there are any financial schemes to help with moving expenses.

ELIGIBILITY CRITERIA FOR RETIREMENT HOUSING

Each council and housing association sets eligibility criteria for its retirement housing. To be eligible your relative would need to be able to show that he or she:

- Has a need for housing as described in the council's allocation policy (see below).
- Has a need for the support and facilities offered by retirement housing.
- Has reached the minimum age, usually 55, or 60, occasionally 50.
- Has the ability to live independently with or without care services.
- Has some degree of housing need because of the physical condition of his or her present home; or
- Has medical and/or social reasons for wanting to move, such as poor health, disabilities, loneliness, fear or isolation from friends and family; and
- Is not easily able to buy rather than rent; and
- If he or she is not living locally already and has good reason for wanting to move to the area applied for, such as being nearer family or close friends.

Allocation policies

The local council's housing policy sets out which groups of people are given priority ('reasonable preference') in the allocation of properties. These groups include people:

Northern Ireland

To apply for permanent accommodation through the Northern Ireland Housing Executive (NIHE), your relative must have a substantial local connection. For example, he or she must:

- Be living in Northern Ireland.
- Have lived in Northern Ireland in the past.
- Need to live in Northern Ireland to receive family support.

If your relative wants to apply for rented retirement housing in Northern Ireland, he or she should contact the Northern Ireland Housing Executive (NIHE) (see below) or a housing association for an application form, complete the form and return it to the NIHE. NIHE will then assess your relative's personal circumstances and allocate points according to their need. NIHE will then put your relative's name on the waiting list and accommodation will be offered to the applicant with the highest number of points.

For more detailed information about renting retirement housing in Northern Ireland, go to www.nihe.gov.uk.

- Who are homeless and are considered to be vulnerable.
- Owed a statutory duty by the council due to other action taken, such as compulsory purchase orders.

- Occupying unsanitary or overcrowded accommodation, such as sharing a bathroom with another household.
- Who need to move on medical or welfare grounds.
- Who need to move to a particular area or would otherwise face hardship.

COMMON HOUSING REGISTER

Local councils and most housing associations in England, Wales and Scotland work together and often have a common housing register for applicants in their local area. This means that if your relative applies to the council for housing, his or her name will be placed on a local common housing register and, subject to eligibility and wishes, he or she will be considered for housing from both the council and local housing associations.

Your relative could also ask the council whether there are any housing associations (such as Abbeyfield Houses – see page 101) in their area that keep their own waiting lists. If there are, it is worth your relative contacting them to check the eligibility criteria.

CHOICE-BASED LETTINGS

A number of local councils and the housing associations with whom they work are now setting up choice-based lettings schemes. The council advertises

vacant properties on a website and/or produces a news sheet and anyone whose name is on the housing waiting list can put in a request for a property hat meets their needs. The property is let to the bidder with the highest priority.

Retirement housing is sometimes included in choice-based letting schemes and if this is the case, the local council will tell your relative about it when they register for housing. The Government's target is for all areas to introduce choice-based lettings by 2010.

HOUSING TRANSFERS

If your relative is looking for retirement housing and is already a council or housing association tenant, he or she should approach the local housing officer who will explain how to apply for a transfer to retirement housing. They may also tell your relative about any **mutual exchange schemes** they run. There is also a web-based exchange scheme called Homeswapper, which allows social housing tenants to post exchange requests (see box below).

Jargon buster

Mutual exchange schemes Allow council and housing association tenants to exchange homes with the permission of their landlord

---

For more information about choice-based lettings, go to www.communities.gov.uk/housing/housingmanagementcare/choicebasedlettings. To find out more about Homeswapper, visit www.homeswapper.co.uk.

CHARGES FOR SOCIAL HOUSING

If your relative rents retirement housing from a housing association or the local council where there is a scheme manager and/or an emergency alarm, there is likely to be a rent and service charge and a housing support charge. The landlord is responsible for telling your relative how much the charges are and what services they cover.

Rent and service charge

This covers the housing management costs, such as rent, upkeep of the communal areas and lift maintenance. If your relative is on a low income and has little capital, Housing Benefit (see page 32) can help pay for the rent and service charge.

Housing support charge

The housing support charge covers the services provided by the scheme manager and/or emergency alarm. If your relative is receiving full or partial Housing Benefit, the Supporting People fund (see below) will pay all the housing support charge. All that will be needed for the housing support charge to be paid is confirmation to the local Supporting People team of your relative's entitlement to Housing Benefit. For more information

contact your relative's local council Supporting People team.

Neither the rent and service charge nor the housing support charge cover personal care services, such as help with getting up in the mornings, shopping or preparation of meals, which are provided through the local council following an assessment of your relative's needs.

In social retirement housing there is no reserve fund or ground rent to pay.

Getting financial help

If your relative is considering moving and is concerned about being able to afford the rent, he or she should contact the council's Housing Benefit section with details of the rent and his or her income and savings and ask for a pre-determination (that is how much help they are likely to receive). To find out more details, contact the local CAB, housing advice centre, the scheme manager, housing officer or management organisation.

In Northern Ireland your relative should contact the Northern Ireland Housing Executive district office, who will give advice on the likely amount of their Housing Benefit.

For Supporting People in England, go to www.spkweb.org.uk; for Wales, go to www.housing.wales.gov.uk; for Scotland, go to www.scotland.gov.uk/Topics/Built-environment/Housing/Supportpeople; for Northern Ireland, go to www.nihe.gov.uk/sp.

Leasehold retirement housing

Most leaseholders in retirement housing pay charges to cover the cost of providing the services that are described in the lease and for maintaining the building.

THE MANAGEMENT ORGANISATION

All retirement housing has a management organisation whose job it is to manage the scheme. This may be either a specialist firm appointed by the landlord, or it may be a separate company within the same group of companies as the landlord, or, as in the case of some housing associations, the landlord may also be the management organisation.

In almost all cases, the management organisation works under contract to the landlord and charges a fee for their services. This fee will be reimbursed by the leaseholders through the service charge (see page 129). Remember that the management organisation is usually an agent of the landlord, not of the leaseholders.

If your relative is thinking about buying a leasehold retirement property, he or she may want to find out:

- Whether the management company is a member of the Association of Retirement Housing Managers ARHM (in England only) (see page 147).
- The name of the freeholder. If your relative is thinking of buying a newly built leasehold flat, he or she also needs to ask who will retain the freehold. Once all the properties are sold, some house builders sell the freehold and a change of freeholder may alter the charges for car parking or other communal facilities.
- What the arrangements are for emergency repairs. There should be a 24-hour emergency repair service.
- The names of other nearby schemes that are managed by the management organisation, so that you and your relative can check on its reputation.

❝ Find out who will manage the retirement housing and if they are in the ARHM. ❞

127

❝ In Scotland, the legally binding contract between your relative, owners of other properties and the management organisation is called the Deed of Conditions. ❞

The role of the management organisation

In addition to responsibility for the structure of the block, upkeep of the common areas and provision of the services and facilities described in the lease (Deed of Covenant), the management organisation carries out other duties, some of which are:

- Entering into and managing maintenance contracts.
- Preparing specifications and contracts for minor works and services, such as cleaning.
- Holding annual meetings with leaseholders.
- Recruiting, training and supervising scheme managers.
- Opening and administering bank accounts for the scheme.
- Collecting and accounting for service charges.
- Providing management information to leaseholders.
- Inspecting a property to check its condition and deal with any necessary repairs.
- Recovering unpaid service charges or ground rents or dealing with non-compliance with the lease, including instructing solicitors and giving court evidence.
- Arranging the audit of scheme accounts.

Management organisations that are members of the ARHM are required to publish a list of duties that are included in their management fee and give a copy to all leaseholders.

 For information about the ARHM Code of Practice, go to www.arhm.org.

SERVICE CHARGES IN LEASEHOLD PROPERTIES

The charge covers:

- The cost of the scheme manager (and housing if he or she lives on-site).
- The alarm system and call monitoring centre.
- Communal services, such as the laundry, lounge and garden, outside building maintenance, building insurance.
- The fees charged by the management organisation for their services.

As a general rule, the more services that are provided, the higher the service charge becomes.

Service charges often appear expensive, especially to people who are used to doing their own maintenance. But if your relative adds up the amount spent on services, such as house maintenance and repairs, building insurance, window cleaning and water and sewerage charges as well as considering the lower energy costs of a modern flat, he or she will be able to calculate the difference in cost between running his or her current home and a retirement property, and the service charges may not seem so bad after all.

How the service charge is calculated

The management organisation estimates the total income and expenditure for the coming financial year and calculates the total amount required to run the scheme. This total is then apportioned (divided)

among the leaseholders according to the rules set out in the lease.

There is no standard lease, so the apportionment of the costs can be done in different ways:

- The lease may say that the costs must be shared equally between the flats.
- Or it may say that the costs are shared in fractions or percentages, often based on the size or number of bedrooms. For example, one-bedroom flats pay 2.9 per cent and two-bedroom flats pay 3.5 per cent of the total charge.

Signing the lease signifies agreement to the way the service charge is apportioned between properties.

Service charge calculations can be complex as can the fact that the service charge is initially calculated on an estimate of the total cost of running the scheme for the forthcoming financial year and then adjusted at the end of the financial year in light of the actual expenditure. The profit/loss is then either refunded to the leaseholders or carried forward to the next year's service charge account.

❝ The apportionment of the service charge between flats can be done in different ways as there is no standard lease. ❞

Leaseholders have a right to a summary of all service charge income and expenditure within six months of the end of the accounting year. If it is felt that some of the costs are unreasonable, leaseholders have the right to challenge the service charge at a Leasehold Valuation Tribunal (LVT) (see box on page 133). But before doing this, there are other ways such as using the management organisation's complaints procedure or considering mediation to deal with the problem.

The charges are usually paid annually, but they can sometimes be paid half yearly or quarterly.

> **“Leaseholders have a right to a summary of all service charge income and expenditure after the accounting year end. ”**

Reserve fund

A reserve fund (sometimes also called a sinking fund) is money set aside to pay for large items of expenditure, such as renewing the lift, painting the outside of the building or replacing the central heating. It is set up so that leaseholders are not suddenly faced with big bills for major expenditure. In setting up the reserve fund, like other services, the management organisation must follow the provisions in the lease.

Leaseholders pay into the reserve fund through their service charges, but some retirement housing leases specify that the management organisation should deduct a percentage of the sale price as a contribution to the reserve fund. This may be instead of, or in addition to the regular contribution.

Service charge rules

Your relative's lease (Deed of Condition in Scotland) will require him or her to pay variable service charges (charges that vary each year based on the actual or estimated cost of the services). Various Landlord and Tenant Acts and the Leasehold Reform Act 2002 set out the basic ground rules for service charges, defining what is considered a service charge, requirements for reasonableness and for prior consultation with leaseholders.

- The service charges must be reasonable and may be challenged at the Leasehold Valuation Tribunal (LVT) (see box, page 133). Most leases allow the management organisation to recover their costs for managing the scheme, providing the services described in the lease, for maintenance, repair and upkeep of the building and for contributions to the reserve fund. The management organisation is reimbursed for their expenditure but should not make a profit from the management. Where the management organisation seeks

Service charge timetable

Assuming the management organisation's financial year runs from 1 April to 31 March, the timetable for discussions and meetings about the service charge will be:

Time	Meetings/discussions
November before the start of the financial year	• Estimate for the budget for forthcoming financial year sent to all leaseholders
December	• Management organisation's representative (often the area housing officer) meets leaseholders at the scheme to explain figures and consult on the proposed budget • The final service charge figure for the next year is set after the meeting
January/February	• Final budget and notification of service charges are sent to all leaseholders together with a breakdown of the Supporting People (see page 126) costs
March	• Service charge invoices sent out to leaseholders
July-September	• Accounts for the preceding financial year are finalised, the actual cost of running the services is established and arrangements made to deal with profit/loss on service charge account

to make a profit, they must make sure that the lease includes the necessary provision.

• The law also expects the management organisation to behave in a reasonable manner with regard to expenditure on the building. However, the freeholder and, on his or her behalf, the management organisation has a long-term interest in maintaining the value of his or her investment, while the leaseholder may have a much shorter view, only intending to remain in the property for a few years. Disputes are often caused by the difference between these two views.

• Leaseholders must be consulted before the management organisation authorises expenditure on major works that will cost any leaseholder more than £250 in service charges, or enters into a long-term agreement. These are agreements for contracts that are for more than 12 months, such as a lift-maintenance contract lasting three years, and would cost each leaseholder more than £100 a year in service charge. However,

131

Case Study — Mr William Lowrey

Mr Lowrey was 89 when he moved into a newly built leasehold retirement housing scheme in north London. When he received his first service charge demand he queried the fact that it included an amount to build up the reserve fund, which was to pay for major items of future expenditure, such as replacement of the lift. He reasoned that he would not still be living in his flat when the lift needed renewing and therefore he did not need to pay this element of the service charge. He raised the issue with the management organisation, then with his solicitor – they both said he had to pay. He then contacted the Advice, Information and Mediation Service (AIMS) and the Association of Retirement Housing Managers (ARHM) (see page 147), who both explained that signing the lease signified his agreement to the lease and that the management organisation had a duty to plan for the long-term viability of the building. Eventually Mr Lowrey paid, but he didn't give up on the grumbling.

leaseholders can only comment, suggest a contractor and know what estimates have been obtained, but the management organisation can decide not to accept the leaseholders' views.

If the management organisation fails to use the correct procedures to carry out the consultation, it will be unable to recover the costs of the work from leaseholders beyond the statutory limits of £100 and £250 per flat.

- **The management organisation is required to provide copies of at least two estimates** for the work, with at least one of them being from someone with no connection to the management organisation.

Leaseholders have the right to comment on the proposals and to suggest alternative contractors or nominate a contractor for consideration. Once again, though, it is consultation only – in the end, the management organisation can decide not to accept the leaseholders' views.

- **If the management organisation considers the work too urgent** to wait for the consultation with leaseholders, it must apply to a LVT for permission to carry out the work.
- **All demands for service charges must be in writing** and must contain the management organisation's name and address. If the address is not in

For more information about leaseholders' rights, see page 141. For more details about LVTs, visit www.lease-advice.org.

England or Wales, the notification must give an address in England or Wales at which notices may be served by the leaseholder. Normally the lease requires the service charge to be paid in advance, but any service charge demand that relates to completion of work must be issued within 18 months of the date the management organisation incurred the cost.

- Service charges should be held in trust.
- The management organisation must account for all annual expenditure through a summary of relevant costs following a written request from a leaseholder or the secretary of a recognised residents' association. After the summary has been provided, a leaseholder or secretary of a recognised residents' association can inspect the relevant documents.

> **!** Unless your relative's lease has a 'sweeping-up' clause (a clause that covers general services not specifically mentioned elsewhere), they should only pay for services specifically mentioned in the lease.

❝In Scotland, specific information about services, service charges, consultation rights and dispute resolution is in the Deed of Conditions.❞

Leasehold Valuation Tribunal (LVT)

Both landlords and leaseholders have a right to ask a Leasehold Valuation Tribunal (LVT) whether a charge or proposed charge is 'reasonable'. However, as there is no statutory definition of what is reasonable, the LVT will consider the evidence presented and then make a determination on the matter. The LVT may also determine:

- Whether the service charge is payable under the lease.
- By whom and to whom it is payable.
- The date on which it is payable.
- The manner of payment.

To find the local Citizens Advice Bureau, visit www.adviceguide.org.uk. To find the local Age Concern in England, visit www.ageconcern.org.uk; in Scotland, www.ageconcernscotland.org.uk; in Wales, www.accymru.org.uk; and in Northern Ireland, www.ageconcernni.org or tel: 028 9024 5799.

Help with service charges

If your relative receives Pension Credit, he or she is likely to be able to get help with the service charge and the housing related support charge (the services provided by the scheme manager and the emergency alarm). Your relative should contact the Pension Service and ask them to reassess his or her entitlement. Your relative should also contact the Supporting People administering authority (see page 126) who will make a payment towards the housing related support element of the service charge.

The scheme manager or housing officer will be able to give your relative details of contacts, as will the local Citizens Advice Bureau or Age Concern.

Ground rent

In addition to service charges, leaseholders have to pay ground rents. Ground rents are fees paid by the leaseholder to the management organisation – historically for the land on which the property stood. The details will be in the lease. Some retirement housing has peppercorn ground rent – no money is required (see page 139). However, many have ground rents that are high compared with non-age-exclusive properties.

The lease will set out how much the ground rent is, when it should be paid and when it will be reviewed. Some ground rents in retirement housing are reviewed, for example, every 21 or 25 years and the charge may be linked to the retail prices index (RPI). If this is the case, the increase could be steep. This is a particular issue for retirement housing that was built around 25 years ago as it may be coming up for a ground rent review shortly.

" Those who receive Pension Credit should be able to get help to pay the service charge and the housing related support charge. "

For more information about ground rents and ground rent reviews, go to page 137.

Leases and tenancy agreements

Leases and tenancy agreements can be long and complex documents. This chapter explains some of the things to look out for when buying leasehold retirement housing. It also explains the essentials of tenancy agreements.

Learning about leases

A lease is the contract between the freeholder (landlord) and the leaseholder, giving the leaseholder the right to live in the flat for a specific number of years subject to the payment of ground rent.

A new flat is often sold with a 99- or 125-year lease (999 years or longer in Northern Ireland). The length of time remaining on the lease decreases with each successive buyer, which means that if the initial purchaser had a 99-year lease and lived in the flat for five years, the next purchaser would buy the flat with 94 years remaining on the lease.

The lease sets out the responsibilities of the landlord and the leaseholder. Houses and bungalows in retirement housing are usually sold freehold with a separate agreement covering the provision of services, such as the scheme manager and the emergency alarm.

Normally the landlord undertakes to ensure the leaseholder has 'quiet enjoyment' (see table, page 139) of the flat and is responsible for the maintenance and repair of the structure of the building and the provision of the services that are set out in the lease.

The leaseholder is responsible for reimbursing the costs of these services to the management organisation through the service charges.

LEASEHOLD VERSUS FREEHOLD OWNERSHIP

If your relative is thinking of moving from a house to a leasehold retirement flat, he or she may want to think about the differences in ownership. Your relative is probably used to being responsible for all the repairs, maintenance and upkeep of the house and garden. But in a retirement flat there will be restrictions on what leaseholders can do with their flats, and the management organisation will be responsible for the upkeep of the block and the communal areas. Most older people are glad to relinquish this responsibility, but it may require some re-adjustment.

Leases are complex and often very long. They are used in England, Wales and Northern Ireland, but in Scotland all property is freehold and the Deed of Conditions lays down the terms under which the property is purchased. A lease attempts to describe who does what and also to set rules for everything that may happen in the next 100 years or so.

There is no standard lease in retirement housing – they are all

For more information about freeholds, see the *Which? Essential Guide: Buy, Sell and Move House.*

different. It is, therefore, very important that you and your relative read and understand the lease and get legal advice if there is anything you do not understand. Any problems must be sorted out before contracts are exchanged.

> **"In a retirement flat there will be restrictions on what leaseholders can do with their flats. ""**

RETIREMENT HOUSING LEASES

In addition to the clauses found in most leases (Deed of Conditions), retirement housing leases include some unusual clauses that your relative will need to be aware of.

Age restrictions

Almost all retirement housing leases restrict the age at which someone can live in the property (see page 95).

Pets

An increasing number of leases allow pets; usually with the permission of the management organisation. But some do not allow dogs or cats in blocks of flats with lifts. If your relative wants to take his or her pet to the new home, your relative needs to ensure that there is written permission from the management organisation. Special arrangements can often be made for assistance dogs.

Ground rents

Ground rents in retirement housing have traditionally been higher than in other types of leasehold housing. Ground rents can vary considerably and the lease should set out how much ground rent is payable, when it has to be paid, when it will be reviewed and the mechanism for calculating increases (see page 134).

Ground rent reviews

Some leases allow the ground rent to increase by fixed amounts during the life of the lease, such as £100 for the first 21 years, £200 for the next 21 years. But some may link the increase to an index, such as the retail prices index (RPI) (see page 134).

Subletting

While some leases do not allow any subletting, others will allow subletting but give the management organisation authority to charge a fee for giving their permission.

Rental of the scheme manager's accommodation

Some retirement housing leases state that the management organisation may

For advice on leases, go to LEASE at www.lease-advice.org.uk. See also AIMS (www.ageconcern.org.uk/aims) and Shelter at http:// england.shelter.org.uk; http://northernireland.shelter.org.uk; http://scotland.shelter.org.uk and www.sheltercymru.org.uk.

charge for the scheme manager's accommodation and that this charge will be passed on to the leaseholders through the service charge. This means that big increases in property prices can cause increases in the service charge.

Parking

Most retirement housing has less parking than the number of flats. Most leases do not allocate specific parking spaces to particular flats but those that do may make an extra charge. Some leases allow the management organisation to charge if it wishes, so the arrangements may change if a new management organisation is appointed. If parking is important to your relative, he or she should ask if the lease allows for charging and whether there is any intention to do so.

Re-sale restrictions and charges

Almost all retirement housing leases have restrictions on re-sale. Your relative should be clear whether the lease has to be surrendered (given up), or whether it is assignable and whether the management organisation has nomination rights.

- **Surrendering a lease:** A few leases require the leaseholder to surrender the lease to the management organisation and the amount the management organisation pays them for the lease is usually quoted as a percentage of the price paid on purchase. The management organisation then takes over the task of finding a buyer for the property.
- **Assigning a lease:** Most leases are assignable, which means that your relative can sell the lease to the next buyer within the conditions set out in the lease.
- **Nomination rights:** Some leases give the management organisation the right to nominate a buyer and charge a fixed price, perhaps 1 or 2 per cent of the sale price for this service. Other leases give the management organisation nomination rights for a fixed period, perhaps a month, after which the leaseholder can advertise the property in the normal way.
- **Re-sale charges:** Retirement leases often contain clauses permitting charges on re-sale. One common clause is a charge of 1 per cent of the sale price, in return for providing the seller's solicitor with the information needed to sell the property.

❝ Most retirement housing leases have restrictions on re-sale. ❞

For more information about leases, see the *Which? Essential Guide* to *Renting and Letting* and the Leasehold Advisory Service (LEASE) at www.lease-advice.org.uk (England and Wales).

Leasehold definitions

- **Assignment** The sale of a lease to another person
- **Covenant** A promise or undertaking between the landlord and leaseholder, for example, the leaseholder agrees to pay the service charge
- **Demised premises** The property that is the subject of the lease, such as the flat
- **Easements** Rights granted to the leaseholder over other flats in the same block, for example, right of access to next door if needed for repairs
- **Forfeiture** The means by which the landlord can bring a lease to an early end if the leaseholder fails to keep to the conditions of the lease (this is severely restricted by law)
- **Freehold** The absolute ownership of property until the end of time or the sale of it
- **Ground rent** Sum payable annually by the leaseholder to the landlord in addition to the service charge
- **Leaseholder** The person who buys a flat with a lease; also known as lessee
- **Parties** The landlord and the leaseholder named in the lease
- **Peppercorn** Notional ground rent – nothing to pay
- **Premium** The capital sum paid to buy the lease – the purchase price of the flat
- **Provisos** The part of the lease containing administrative conditions, the most common of these is forfeiture
- **Quiet enjoyment** A promise by the landlord not to interfere unlawfully with the leaseholder's enjoyment of the flat, such as by not turning up unannounced or interfering with the leaseholder's possessions
- **Recitals** The part of the lease stating the basic facts, title number, names of landlord and leaseholder
- **Reservations** Rights being kept by the landlord over the flat that is being sold, for example, a right of access if the landlord needs it to carry out structural repairs
- **Reserved property** The parts of the block that are not owned by any leaseholders and are the landlord's responsibility, such as communal areas and gardens
- **Schedule** Appendix. For example, a description of the premises may be included as schedule 1 (appendix 1)
- **Subletting or under-letting** Where the leaseholder grants a sub- or under-lease of the property to a tenant or sub-tenant
- **Surrender** The selling back or giving up of the lease by the leaseholder to the landlord
- **Term** Period of time for which the lease is granted usually 99 or 125 years
- **Yield up** Giving back, usually to the landlord

Questions to ask a solicitor about the lease

It is important that either your relative or you check a lease with a solicitor before signing. Here are some questions for your relative (or you on his or her behalf) to ask.

- Has the management organisation sent you a leaseholder's handbook or information pack that explains things in plain English and, if so, can I see it?

- What is the name of the freeholder (landlord)?

- What is the name of the management organisation?

- How many years remain on the lease?

- What is the minimum age for living in and buying this property?

- How much is the ground rent; when does it have to be paid; when will it next be reviewed; and what criteria are used to calculate the increase?

- How much is the service charge; what does it include; how is it calculated; how often is it paid; and how is it apportioned between properties?

- Is the current owner up-to-date with his or her service charge payments and might there be a deficit on the service charge account at the end of the financial year? If these debts are not paid, will they become my legal responsibility? (The usual way of dealing with this is for your relative's solicitor to keep back part of the purchase price until these matters are finalised.)

- Can I keep a pet?

- Can I sublet the property and will the management organisation charge for giving its approval?

- Are any charges to be paid on selling the property and, if there are, how much are they and what do they cover?

- Can I obtain a mortgage (see pages 109–10) or equity release product (see page 79) if necessary?

- Can I make changes to the flat, such as replacing the bathroom, if I want to?

- What actions might the management organisation take if I become frail and unable to cope living by myself?

Clauses relating to the ability to live an independent life

Some leases have clauses that would allow the management organisation to terminate the lease if the leaseholder became incapable of living an independent life. Most modern leases do not include these clauses and where such clauses do occur they are probably not enforceable.

If difficulties arise, most management organisations will attempt to offer advice and assistance to leaseholders and their families to try to ensure the leaseholder receives the help and support they need.

A LEASEHOLDER'S RIGHTS

The law relating to leasehold is complex and subject to change. If your relative needs further information or advice, it is important he or she contacts a specialist advice agency such as those listed in the box, below.

Extending a lease

A leaseholder has the right to extend his or her lease at any time. This can be expensive and is only worth considering if your relative's flat is reducing in value because of the short lease. The new lease will run for 90 years after the end of the existing lease and will be a peppercorn ground rent (see page 139).

Amending a lease

Leases can be amended at any time with the agreement of all the parties concerned. If agreement cannot be reached, there are occasions when an application can be made to an LVT (see page 133), such as a challenge to the service charge. However, such an application must be supported by at least 75 per cent of leaseholders and not opposed by more than 10 per cent. This means that an individual leaseholder is unlikely to be able to change any of the contentious clauses in their lease.

" Termination clauses if the leaseholder cannot live independently are not really enforceable. "

Specialist advice agencies

- **The Leasehold Advisory Service (LEASE): www.lease-advice.org.uk.** Provides free advice and guidance to leaseholders in England and Wales on all aspects of leasehold law.
- **Advice, Information and Mediation Service (AIMS): www.ageconcern.org.uk/aims** (England and Wales) or http://northernireland.shelter.org.uk (Northern Ireland).
- **The Association of Retirement Housing Managers (ARHM): www.arhm.org.**

For more information about AIMS and ARHM, see page 147.

Tenancy agreements

The tenancy is a legal agreement between your relative and his or her landlord. It gives your relative the right to live in the accommodation in exchange for paying rent to the landlord.

The law only requires your relative to have a tenancy agreement if his or her tenancy is to last for more than three years. But it is always a good idea to request one. The tenancy agreement lists the terms and conditions your relative and the landlord should adhere to.

Tenancy agreements can be either written or verbal, but your relative should always insist on having a written agreement and should always read it carefully and ensure he or she understands it before signing the agreement and moving in. Your relative should seek advice from a housing advice centre or independent advice service, such as CAB or Shelter if it is unclear (see below).

TYPES OF TENANCY

There are various types of tenancy depending on the wording of the tenancy agreement, whether the landlord is a local council, housing association or private landlord, and when the tenancy started. If your relative is in any doubt as to the type of his or her tenancy, he or she should check with Shelter, a local CAB or housing advice centre.

Council tenants

Council tenants may have:

- **An introductory tenancy.** This is a 12-month trial tenancy, which gives most of the rights of a secure tenancy, but introductory tenants can be evicted much more easily than secure tenants. The most common reasons for eviction are that your relative has caused nuisance to neighbours, has not paid the rent, has regularly paid it late, or has moved out and let the property to someone else. Not all councils run introductory tenancy schemes but if they do, the scheme must apply to all new tenants.

❝A written tenancy agreement is always desirable.❞

 The Shelter websites are: for England, http://england.shelter.org.uk; for Wales, www.sheltercymru.org.uk; for Scotland, http://scotland.shelter.org.uk; and for Northern Ireland, http://northernireland.shelter.org.uk.

- **A secure tenancy.** At the end of an introductory tenancy, your relative should automatically become a secure tenant as long as he or she has not broken the tenancy agreement. Most council tenants have secure tenancies; which means they have the right to live in their homes indefinitely and can only be evicted following a court order.

Housing association tenants

Housing association tenants may have:

- **A starter tenancy.** This is a 12-month trial tenancy. The starter tenancy gives fewer rights from eviction. The most common reasons for eviction are not paying the rent, causing a nuisance to neighbours, using the property for

Tenancies in Scotland and Northern Ireland

In Scotland

Council and housing association tenants will usually have a Scottish secure tenancy agreement (SST) or, less frequently, a short Scottish secure tenancy (SSST).

Private tenants usually have an assured or short assured tenancy, which have slight differences from the English versions such as:
- Both have the right to a written tenancy agreement.
- Both will automatically renew after the end of the fixed term unless the landlord gives written notice.

In Northern Ireland
- Northern Ireland Housing Executive tenants may have secure tenancies or introductory tenancies (for all new tenancies). Introductory tenancies automatically become secure tenancies unless the housing association has started eviction proceedings.
- Housing association tenants may have secure tenancies, unsecure (which give similar rights to uncontrolled private tenants) tenancies or introductory tenancies (for the first 12 months). Introductory tenancies automatically become secure tenancies unless the housing association has started eviction proceedings.
- Some private tenants may have protected tenancies, so they can only be evicted by their landlord for specific legal reasons. Most private tenancies in Northern Ireland fall under the category of all other tenancies. These tenancies have the right to have a rent book and freedom from illegal eviction. All other rights and responsibilities should be outlined in the tenancy agreement.

More information about tenancies in Scotland, go to http://Scotland.shelter.org.uk. For Northern Ireland, go to http://northernireland.shelter.org.uk.

The tenancy agreement

All written tenancy agreements should include information such as:

- The name of the tenant(s).

- The address of the property being rented.

- The name and address of the management organisation, landlord and letting agent (if there is one).

- The rent being charged, when it is due and how it should be paid and what it covers.

- The length of the agreement.

- The amount of deposit required, what it covers and in what circumstances it will not be returned (see below).

- Whether your relative can leave before the end of his or her tenancy and if so, the amount of notice that must be given. If your relative signs a tenancy agreement for a fixed period, say, six months, it is likely that he or she will have to pay the rent for the whole period, even if leaving earlier.

- What furniture, if any, will be provided.

- Who is responsible for repairs (the management organisation/landlord is always responsible for external and structural repairs). If your relative is responsible for internal alterations or improvements, he or she will probably want a clause in the agreement that allows internal alterations to be carried out, even though these are likely to be subject to agreement from the management organisation.

- Whether your relative can sublet or have anyone to stay long term.

- Whether your relative can keep a pet. If your relative has a pet, he or she should have written permission for the pet to stay in the flat before moving in.

- Whether there are any other rules, for example, about smoking or guests.

Deposits

A deposit of the equivalent of four to six weeks' rent is usually required. From April 2007, all deposits taken by landlords and lettings agents for assured shorthold tenancies must be protected by a tenancy deposit protection scheme. These allow tenants to get all or part of their deposit back when they are entitled to it and includes a free dispute resolution service. For more information see www.direct.gov.uk.

illegal activities and subletting without the housing association's permission.

- **An assured tenancy.** At the end of a starter tenancy, your relative should automatically become an assured tenant unless the housing association has started proceedings to evict your relative. Assured tenants have the right to live in their homes as long as they do not break the conditions of their tenancy agreement. The housing association must have a court order to evict your relative.

- **A secure tenancy.** Most housing association tenants who moved into their accommodation before 15 January 1989 will have secure tenancies, which means they have the right to live in their homes indefinitely and can only be evicted following a court order.

Tenants in privately rented retirement housing

In privately rented retirement housing, tenants may have:

- **An assured shorthold tenancy.** These are the most common tenancies in most private residential lets. They are issued for a fixed term such as six months and give the landlord the right to repossess at the end of the term.

- **An assured tenancy.** This gives your relative fairly strong rights against eviction – the landlord must have a legal reason to evict (such as non-payment of rent) and obtain a court order and a possession order.

WHAT IS A LICENCE?

Most people who live in rented accommodation have a tenancy, but some will have a licence. The distinction is not defined in law and if your relative is unsure whether he or she has a tenancy or licence, you should seek advice from CAB, Shelter or a housing advice centre. A licence gives:

- **Your relative permission to occupy the premises** with limited security of tenure. This means your relative's landlord could ask him or her to leave at any time by giving him or her 'reasonable' notice.

- **The landlord the right to enter your relative's premises,** for example, for cleaning, provided that 'reasonable notice' is given.

If your relative has been offered a licence to occupy accommodation, he or she needs to know what services are provided, when they are provided, under what circumstances the landlord will enter your relative's home and whether there are any restrictions on the use of communal areas or the amount of time your relative can spend away from the accommodation.

66 A licence gives your relative permission to occupy the premises with limited security and he or she could be asked to leave at any time. 99

If things go wrong

For most people living in retirement housing, the experience is a positive one, but sometimes problems do occur. Living in a block of flats, in close proximity to your neighbours and having to pay for things that, as a householder your relative may have previously carried out for him- or herself, can sometimes lead to misunderstandings and difficulties.

If problems do arise, there are a number of services that can help (see opposite). Most organisations have complaints procedures, there are independent advice agencies (some providing mediation and appropriate dispute resolution), the ombudsman service and – if all else fails – the courts.

BEFORE USING THE COMPLAINTS PROCEDURE

If possible, your relative should first try to talk to the person concerned – perhaps the scheme manager or housing officer. This gives him or her the chance to try to sort out your relative's concerns at an early stage. Before talking to that person, your relative should:

- **Be clear what the complaint is,** why he or she is complaining and whether the complaint is addressed to the right organisation, for example, whether it is about the housing or the care services provided through the local council.
- **Gather all the paperwork about the problem.** This may include his or her lease/tenancy agreement and any letters he or she has received.
- **Put his or her complaint in writing.** Although your relative shouldn't necessarily have to do this, it is often a good idea to do so and keep a copy. Your relative should also make notes of any telephone conversations, including names, dates and contact numbers for the people spoken to.
- **Think about the desired result** of the complaint. For example, does your relative want an apology or compensation (if, for instance, the heating did not work for several days).

A complaint should ideally be made by the person who has the problem. However, if your relative is making it on

Information about residents' associations and how they are run is given on pages 100-1.

behalf of someone else, he or she should make sure the other person agrees to the action.

WHO CAN HELP WITH A COMPLAINT?

There are various organisations and charities that your relative can turn to get help with a complaint.

The Association of Retirement Housing Managers (ARHM)

In England, many management organisations of retirement housing are members of the ARHM. The ARHM's aim is to promote high standards of practice and ethics in the management of retirement housing nd the association has a government approved Code of Practice (see box below).

If your relative's management organisation is a member of ARHM, you can ask ARHM to investigate alleged breaches of the Code of Practice once your relative has been through the management organisation's complaints procedure (see page 148). The Code of Practice can also be used in evidence at a Leasehold Valuation Tribunal (LVT) (see page 133) when considering whether a management organisation has been effective according to reasonable standards.

The advantages of group action

Management problems in retirement housing can often be more effectively raised through a recognised residents' association or possibly a residents' forum if one is available. If there is no recognised residents' association, your relative may find it helpful to have the support of neighbours.

❝ The aim of ARHM is to promote high standards of practice in retirement housing management. ❞

Advice Information and Mediation Service (AIMS)

AIMS is part of Age Concern England (and also has a remit for Wales) and runs an information and advice service that can offer your relative independent advice on any retirement housing matter such as disputes between neighbours and issues involving the scheme manager.

AIMS also run a mediation/appropriate dispute resolution (ADR) service, which can prove particularly useful where people have an ongoing relationship, such as residents and scheme managers. Mediation is voluntary and is based on the mediator meeting both parties separately and then together so that each party has the chance to put their points and to listen to arguments raised by others.

 ARHM information is to be found at www.arhm.org. For more information about AIMS, go to www.ageconcern.org.uk/aims (England and Wales) or www.ageconcernscotland.org.uk (Retirement Housing Advice Service, Scotland). For housing rights in Northern Ireland, go to http://northernireland.shelter.org.uk.

Leases and tenancy agreements

147

THE MANAGEMENT ORGANISATION'S COMPLAINTS PROCEDURE

All management organisations have a complaints procedure, which is available to all leaseholders. This is sometimes in the residents' handbook and sometimes on a separate sheet. If your relative does not have a copy, he or she should ask the scheme manager or management organisation. This procedure will state who your relative should complain to and what to do if the complaint is not resolved at the first stage. Most complaints procedures have three or four stages.

REFERRAL TO AN OMBUDSMAN

If your relative has been through all the stages of the management organisation's complaints procedure and he or she is still not satisfied, the problem can be referred to the local government ombudsman (see page 204) or the Housing Ombudsman Service.

Housing Ombudsman Service (HOS)

All housing associations registered with the Housing Corporation must be members of HOS and some other management organisations subscribe voluntarily to the service as well. To find out whether your relative's management organisation subscribes to HOS, he or she can either ask the management organisation or check with HOS direct.

The Housing Ombudsman deals with complaints about the way housing is managed, but only after a complainant has been through all the stages of the management organisation's complaints procedure. The Housing Ombudsman may initially be able to resolve the matter through informal contact with the management organisation; they may also recommend mediation, but where they consider it appropriate, they will carry out a more formal investigation. This is a thorough investigation using the service's own staff to investigate the complaint.

At the end of the investigation, the Ombudsman writes to both the complainant and the management organisation explaining the findings, whether mal-administration has occurred and what should be done about it. They may recommend that an apology is made, compensation paid, remedial action taken or changes made to procedures.

❝ You have to go through all the stages of the management organisation's complaints procedure first. ❞

 For information about HOS in England, visit www.ihos.org.uk; for Wales, visit www.ombudsman-wales.org.uk; for Scotland, visit www.spso.org.uk, and for Northern Ireland, visit: www.ni-ombudsman.org.uk.

Finding a care home

It has been government policy for some years now to encourage care to be delivered to people in their own homes, rather than in care homes. But sometimes moving into a care home is the only remaining option available. The reasons for this are varied, but normally it would be because the care needs associated with your relative's condition can no longer be met at home.

The care home spectrum

If your relative has decided that moving into a care home is the right choice, it is important that moving becomes a positive step, even if a home is needed at short notice or vacancies to meet your relative's specific needs and wishes are hard to find.

TYPES OF CARE HOME

Care homes vary in size, in the ways in which they are organised and in the services and facilities they offer. There is a wide variation in prices and it is unwise to assume that the more expensive the care home, the higher the standard of care.

All care homes are registered with the social care registration authority for their country (see opposite) and they have to publicise the level of care they provide and how they will meet each resident's care needs. There are two types of care home for older people.

Care homes providing personal care

These are also sometimes called residential homes, rest homes or retirement homes. They provide care for people who either can no longer stay in their own home, even with the support of carers, family or friends, or are at serious risk to themselves or others if they are left alone for any period of time. Care homes offering personal care provide living accommodation, which is usually a room, possibly en suite, meals, help with personal care, such as dressing, supervision of medication, companionship and someone on call at night. They give care during normal short illnesses but do not provide nursing care.

Care homes providing nursing care

These homes are also sometimes called nursing homes. They provide personal and nursing care for 24 hours a day for people who are bedridden, very frail or

---

Elderly mentally ill or elderly mentally infirm homes (EMIs)

Some care homes, registered either for personal care or nursing care, are also registered to provide services to specific categories of older people, such as those diagnosed with dementia. These used to be known as EMI (elderly mentally ill or elderly mentally infirm) homes. However, not all residents with dementia live in care homes that are registered for dementia.

Care homes for people with specific needs

Some not-for-profit care homes provide services for older people with specific needs and interests:

- Specific religious needs, such as Jewish or Catholic.
- Cultural needs, such as Asian or Chinese.
- Specific languages, such as Polish or Gujerati.
- Specific professions, such as retired nurses or retired employees from the wine and spirit trade.
- Females only.
- Specific interests, such as Freemasons or people from the armed services.

These homes may have special criteria describing who they can admit. For more information visit: www.HousingCare.org.

have a medical condition or illness that means they need regular attention from a nurse. There is always a qualified nurse on duty.

Some care homes may have a specific number of beds registered for personal care, and other beds registered for nursing care; some may have a specific number of beds registered for people diagnosed with dementia.

WHO OWNS AND RUNS CARE HOMES?

Care homes are owned and operated in various ways:

- As businesses by private individuals or companies owning groups of homes (sometimes called private homes).
- By not-for-profit organisations, such as housing associations, charities and religious organisations (sometimes called voluntary homes).

- By some local councils, but only care homes providing personal care. Local councils do not own or run care homes that are registered to provide nursing care.

REGISTRATION AND INSPECTION OF CARE HOMES

All care homes have to be registered and inspected by the social care registration authority for their country.

- In England, this is the Commission for Social Care Inspection (CSCI).
- In Wales, the Care and Social Services Inspectorate for Wales (CSSIW).
- In Scotland, the Scottish Commission for the Regulation of Care (Care Commission).
- In Northern Ireland, the Regulation and Quality Improvement Authority (RQIA).

151

The social care registration authorities are independent bodies set up by the Governments to promote improvements in social care and to stamp out bad practice. They inspect all care services in their countries and:

- Register care homes and care agencies to ensure they meet the national minimum standards set by the Department of Health (see page 211).
- Register the people who run the care services and issue registration certificates. They can refuse a registration certificate to prospective candidates who do not meet the legal requirements.
- Keep registers of care services.

Inspection reports and what to look out for

Abridged versions of inspection reports and the star ratings (see box, right) are available on the websites of the social care registration authorities for England, Wales and Scotland (reports for Northern Ireland can be ordered by telephone or email). Reports should also be available at the care home and possibly the local library.

It is always useful to look at inspection reports. In particular:

- **Check the most recent report** and the previous two or three, to see whether points raised by the inspectors have been addressed or whether they reappear on subsequent reports.
- **Check whether high staff turnover** has been mentioned regularly – this could indicate unsettled staff.
- **Note the frequency of inspections.** On the whole, more frequent inspections may denote inspectors' concerns.
- **Note any restrictions** imposed by the inspectors (such as no more admissions of residents with high care needs).

If there is anything you do not understand, ask the care home manager for an explanation.

Star ratings

In May 2008 in England, the Commission for Social Care Inspection (CSCI) introduced 'star ratings'. These are quality ratings for each care home and care service and aim to make it easier to compare the quality of different services. The star ratings are based on inspections of the services and place particular importance on how safe and well managed the service is. Services are rated three-star (excellent), two-star (good), one-star (adequate) and zero stars (poor). More information about the ratings can be found from www.csci.org.uk.

 For more information about each social care registration authority visit www.csci.org.uk (England); www.cssiw.org.uk (Wales); www.carecommission.com (Scotland); www.rqia.org.uk (Northern Ireland).

Admission to a care home

Depending on your relative's health, admission to a care home might take place from hospital or direct from his or her home. The level of funding available will determine the amount of choice you and your relative have.

The local council needs assessment will determine whether your relative meets their criteria and the amount the council will pay; you and your relative may need to think about self-funding or the need for top-up funding.

ADMISSION FROM HOSPITAL

If your relative is in an acute hospital bed, he or she cannot be discharged until his or her medical condition is stable and your relative can safely be moved.

Before discharge, the hospital must notify the local council if they think your relative is likely to need community care services (including a care home), but they must consult your relative before that referral is made. The hospital must notify the council again once a discharge date has been set.

❝Someone in an acute hospital bed cannot be discharged until his or her medical condition is stable and he or she can be safely moved. ❞

If your relative chooses not to have any involvement from the council (either an assessment or services), he or she is then responsible for arranging their own future care.

The discharge process

Step 1 Your relative is given verbal and written information about the discharge process and what to expect.

There may be a ward-based discharge co-ordinator, so if you do not have information about the process, ask ward staff for a name and how to contact that person.

Step 2 Your relative has a legal right to an assessment by NHS and local council staff to see whether any ongoing care is needed after they leave hospital and, if so, what services and who should provide them. If your relative is not able to take part in this assessment, perhaps because of dementia or following a stroke, family and carers should be involved as much as possible.

Step 3 The NHS should decide whether your relative is eligible for any NHS Continuing Healthcare (see page 91).

153

Step 4 The council decides whether your relative is eligible for any help from them. They do this by comparing your relative's assessed needs with the council's eligibility criteria (see page 124).

Step 5 A care plan is drawn up describing how your relative's needs can best be met, including where he or she will live. The care plan should include one or more of the following:

- **Moving from an acute ward** to a non-acute bed in the same hospital or in a community hospital.
- **A period of intermediate care** or rehabilitation services (such as physiotherapy or occupational therapy) if your relative is not yet ready to return home.
- **An interim care package** at home while waiting for a bed in a care home or until any alterations have been made to your relative's home.
- **A temporary stay** in a care home.
- **A care package at home,** including equipment, alterations to the home, carers, community nurses or other NHS staff.

> ❝A care plan describes how your relative's needs can best be met.❞

Choosing a care home

If the local council is paying towards your relative's care, government guidance says your relative can choose any care home as long as:

- **The home meets your relative's assessed needs.**
- **It does not cost more than the council would normally pay for someone with your relative's assessed needs.**
- **The home is willing to enter into a contract with the local council, subject to the council's usual terms and conditions.**
- **The home has a vacancy.**

If there is no care home in the local area that can meet your relative's assessed need, perhaps because one of the assessed needs is to be near his or her family, the council may increase the amount they will pay – see page 168.

- **Going to live with a relative,** with or without support from the local council.
- **Moving into a care home.**

Step 6 The council then carries out a means test to work out how much your relative will have to contribute towards the council arranged services for which he or she has been assessed. If your relative has been assessed as needing

To find out more about the means test, see pages 166-8; and for details about direct payment, see page 77.

Practical arrangements for an effective discharge

- Ensure the hospital have told your relative and (if appropriate) any carers of the date and time of discharge.
- Check the hospital has arranged suitable transport.
- Check the hospital has arranged any medication your relative needs and that he or she knows how often to take it, for how long and how to request further supplies.
- If your relative needs any equipment or continence products, check they are available on the day of discharge and that your relative knows how to use them.
- If your relative is going home, check that the GP has been notified of the discharge date and of any health services your relative will immediately need.
- If your relative is going to a care home, check the care home has been told the date and time of discharge.

services other than residential care, he or she will also be offered a direct payment.

Step 7 After your relative is discharged from the acute ward, the care plan is implemented and monitored.

Interim arrangements

If your relative is ready for discharge and there is no vacancy in his or her chosen care home, interim arrangements may have to be made. Hospital staff, council staff and family members should all be involved in setting up these arrangements, which still have to meet your relative's assessed needs. Interim arrangements could include a move to a non-acute hospital bed or a package of intermediate care in your relative's own home.

It is good practice, where possible, for your relative not to move directly from hospital to a care home for the first time, but to have a period of time at home to make personal arrangements, adjust to his or her new condition and be sure a care home is his or her preferred choice.

Your relative does not have the right to occupy an NHS bed indefinitely but the local council cannot force your relative to go into a care home. The local council has a duty to meet your relative's assessed needs and if he or she does not want to go into a care home, the NHS and council should explore alternative options with you and your relative.

❝Where possible, your relative should have some time at home to make personal arrangements before moving to a care home.❞

155

SELF-FUNDING

If your relative is paying his or her own fees, he or she should always first ask the local council for a needs assessment, then approach the care home of choice and make arrangements directly with them. Your relative will be asked to agree and sign a contract covering such things as the care to be provided, the charges and the terms and conditions of occupancy.

❝ Always ask the local council for a needs assessment even if your relative is paying his or her own fees. ❞

Case Study | Miss Koumei

Miss Koumei was 76 and a retired florist living in a small town just outside London when she had her stroke. When she came out of hospital she could walk slowly and needed some help dressing because her balance was poor. She had lost her confidence and was depressed. Her friends were concerned that she would not be able to manage at home and suggested she went into a nursing home that had just opened in the old manor house not far from where she lived. She sold her house and moved into the nursing home – it was expensive but it felt like living in a hotel. Miss Koumei was much more able than most of the other residents and her friends came to lunch most days.

After six years she realised her money was running out. Local council staff came to assess her needs and told her that she did not need a nursing home and even suggested she would be able to manage living in a retirement flat with some extra services. Miss Koumei was horrified at this suggestion. Eventually, with her friends' help, she used the council's complaints procedure (see pages 201–2) to challenge the assessment and after a lengthy process the council agreed to pay for her to live in a care home providing personal care on the grounds that she had been receiving care for the last six years.

Miss Koumei is also now being encouraged to do more for herself and the council are planning to set up a rehabilitation programme to prepare her for a move to somewhere more suitable in extra care housing.

Finding the right home

For anyone, moving into a care home is a big step and finding the right home is very important. However, it can also be a difficult and time-consuming decision.

WHERE TO START?

If your relative needs a lot of help with his or her daily living and is considering a care home, the first step is to contact the local council and ask for a needs assessment. It is essential this is done if your relative needs any financial help from the council to meet the costs of his or her care. It is also important if your relative is paying for care, because the assessment helps to identify the most appropriate type of care home and will also help your relative to plan ahead if his or her money is likely to run out.

HOW TO FIND A CARE HOME

Each home can only provide the care for which they are registered, so it is a waste of time looking at nursing homes if the council has assessed your relative as needing a care home providing personal care and there is no top-up funding (see page 169) available. The needs assessment will also identify any additional needs, such as for a home registered for people diagnosed with dementia. Your relative will also want to consider whether he or she:

- **Has important lifestyle needs,** such as living in a Jewish home or being able to communicate in a specific language.
- **Wants to live in a specific area.**
- **Has a preference** for a large home that has hotel-like facilities or somewhere that is more homely.

It is unlikely that all your relative's needs and preferences can be met in one care home, so you may have to prioritise, especially if time is short.

Finding a care home in a different area

Your relative can move to a care home anywhere in England, Wales or, by special arrangement, Scotland. In some areas, you may have difficulty finding a vacancy for your relative in a care home

 For more information about the needs assessment, see pages 38-48. Funding a care home is covered in the next chapter on pages 164-94.

at the appropriate cost and that meets his or her needs. For full information on funding implications on choosing a care home, see pages 164–94.

Start your research

Once your relative has decided on the geographical area, get a list of care homes that match the type of home you are seeking:

- **The local council** will have a list of homes in their area.
- **Details of homes in any area** are available from the relevant social care registration authority (see page 151).
- **EAC has a database** of nearly 14,000 care homes in the UK. It also gives details of specialist homes.
- **Independent care advisers** can help identify the most appropriate type of care service and a specific care home. Services and fees are tailored to

individual needs and costs vary between about £100 for an initial telephone interview and advice, to around £550 for a meeting with you and your relative, research into the options and a shortlist of homes within the agreed geographical area.

CONTACTING CARE HOMES

Telephone the care homes to get their brochure and statement of purpose. Depending on who you speak to, it may be useful to tell them if a room is needed urgently and give some indication of your relative's needs. This may save wasting time if, for instance, your relative needs a room in three days' time.

Check the fees, financial arrangements and extra charges regardless of whether the council is paying towards your relative's fees or whether he or she is self-funding. Some care home fees vary

---

Interpreting care home literature

Each home must produce a statement of purpose. Sometimes this document is combined with the latest inspection report and sent out as an information pack. This document is very useful and gives you an idea of the aims and objectives of the home, their philosophy of care, a description of the accommodation, services and facilities, and information about the qualifications of the manager and other staff. Do bear in mind that they are sales documents, so make sure the reality matches the information.

 To find your relative's local council, go to www.direct.gov.uk. The website for the EAC database is www.HousingCare.org. To find an independent care adviser, contact the Association of Independent Care Advisers (AICA) for details of their members: www.aica.org.uk.

according to the amount of care your relative needs and some by the location and size of room.

Once you have read all the information and talked to your relative, make a shortlist of homes you think may be suitable and are within the council's price range (if they are contributing to the funding) or your relative's price range (if he or she is self-funding). The number of homes on your shortlist will depend on the urgency, your time and how specialist are your relative's needs. If you can, take the time to compare several homes.

Visit the homes on your shortlist; depending on the circumstances you may want to visit on your own first to eliminate any unsuitable homes.

THE INITIAL VISIT

Arrange to visit with your relative; talk to the manager, staff and residents and, if possible, stay for a meal. Is the home clean, comfortable and inviting? Is there a fresh, clean smell? Does your relative think that he or she could feel at home there and get on with the other residents?

Although you are assessing the home for your relative's needs (see overleaf for a list of questions to ask), remember, too, that the person showing you around is likely to be 'selling' the home to you and your relative, showing you the best features of the home. The manager will

 If it is impossible for your relative to visit, ask for someone from the home to come to see your relative.

also be assessing your relative, for instance to see if he or she will fit in with the other residents and how much care will be needed. The manager is also likely to be considering what sort of support to your relative you would give and, depending on the ethos of the home, making a judgement about what fees to charge. Many homes charge higher fees to self-funding residents than to council-funded residents.

If you are making a second visit on your own, perhaps before making a final decision, you may want to call into the home without an appointment to see how many visitors are around, how the staff interact with the residents and whether the residents are actively enjoying their care home or just left sitting in their chairs with nothing to do.

Travelling to a home

If your relative has difficulty travelling to visit homes, contact the local Age Concern, Citizens Advice Bureau or Community Transport to see if they have details of transport schemes in your relative's area.

To find your local Age Concern, visit www.ageconcern.org.uk (England); www.accymru.org.uk (Wales); www.ageconcernscotland.org.uk (Scotland); www.ageconcernni.org.uk (Northern Ireland). To find your local CAB, go to www.adviceguide.org.uk.

Questions to ask about care homes

Everyone has different ideas about what they want from a care home. You and your relative may find it useful to look at these questions, find out what your relative thinks is particularly important and then make a list before visiting. Do not be embarrassed about asking lots of questions. If your relative is able to talk to people living in the home, he or she will get an idea of what life is really like.

The location

- What are the surroundings like?
- Is public transport available to reach the home or get out to shops?

Accommodation

- Is it suitable for a wheelchair user? Are there passenger and/or stair lifts?
- Can my relative look at the room he or she may be offered?
- When my relative has been admitted, is he or she likely to have to change rooms?
- Can my relative change rooms if he or she wishes?
- Can my relative bring his or her own possessions and furniture?
- Do bedrooms have TV and telephone points? If not, can my relative make and receive calls in private? What would the charges be?
- Are en-suite facilities available? Are all toilet and washing facilities clean and easily accessible?
- Is there equipment such as grab rails and bath hoists?
- Are pets allowed? Can visitors bring pets into the home?
- Is there a quiet lounge without a television?
- Is there a private room to take visitors?
- Are there gardens in which my relative can sit?
- Can valuables be stored safely, with itemised receipts given?
- Does the home's insurance policy cover loss or damage to my relative's possessions or does cover need arranging?
- Are there smoking and non-smoking areas?
- Is there a bar, or can my relative bring alcohol into the home?
- Can my relative choose when to get up and go to bed?
- Are there regular fire drills?
- What security arrangements are there? Particularly to prevent a resident from wandering out of the home?

Staff

- Do there appear to be enough staff on duty?
- Are the staff friendly, polite and caring? Are they rushing around or do they spend time talking to individual residents?

Care

- Can the home offer suitable care for my relative's needs as outlined in his or her needs assessment?
- Do you have, or can you get, any important items of equipment that my relative needs?
- Can any special needs be met? Including during the night?
- Is there an emergency call system in all the rooms? Is it easy to operate?
- If my relative requires more care in the future, will the home be able to provide this?
- If practical, can my relative's own GP visit? Does a local GP call?
- Are there visiting dentists, opticians?
- Is speech therapy, chiropody, physiotherapy and occupational therapy available? Is there a charge?
- Does the home specialise in providing care for any of the following: Terminal care? Dementia? Physical disability?

Food

- What is the food like? Can we see some menus? Are there choices each day?
- Are meal times flexible?
- Can meals be served in my relative's room?
- Are there facilities for my relative to make a hot drink?

Facilities

- Are visitors welcome at any time? Can they stay for meals? Can they stay overnight?
- What arrangements are made for residents to attend religious services in the home or outside?
- Is there a minibus or other transport? How often is it used and for what?
- How often are social activities, outings and entertainments arranged?

Terms and conditions

- How much are the fees? What do they include? Are they paid in advance or in arrears?
- What isn't included? And how are these items billed?
- How often are the fees reviewed? How much notice is given when fees increase?
- Can you have a specimen copy of the home's contract for residents?

General

- Are there residents' meetings?
- Can my relative have a trial stay?
- Is there a complaints procedure? Do all residents have a copy?
- Is there a waiting list?

IF YOUR RELATIVE NEEDS AN INCREASE IN CARE

If your relative is paying his or her own fees and it is decided that the current care home can't provide the increased level of care, the care home should arrange a review with both you and your relative to talk about the options and plan the next steps. The home should suggest that the local council are asked to assess your relative's needs and recommend a suitable type of home and should also give you local contacts who could help with finding alternative accommodation. The home should give your relative proper notice, as described in their contract.

If the council is contributing to the fees and you feel your relative's needs have increased, talk to the staff in the care home and contact the local council and ask for a re-assessment of your relative's needs. Alternatively, the care home or the GP may do this.

If your relative's needs have increased, it may mean that he or she needs a different type of care home, perhaps one registered for nursing care or dementia. If at all possible, the care home should give sufficient time for alternative arrangements to be made. It is worth asking whether the care home is willing to contact the social care registration authority to seek a special registration for one place, either permanently or until you have time to find another home.

If your relative is in a care home providing nursing care

If your relative receives the NHS Nursing Care Contribution (see page 180), he or she should automatically be re-assessed once a year against the criteria for NHS Continuing Healthcare (see page 91) and to ensure that the nursing care contribution is still required.

IF THE CARE HOME CLOSES

If the care home closes, residents should be given reasonable notice of the closure and, where appropriate, help with finding alternative accommodation. If the council is responsible for contributing to your relative's fees, they have a responsibility for finding suitable alternative accommodation and their first step is usually to re-assess your relative's needs.

If the care home has its registration withdrawn, perhaps because of gross breach of duty, the closure may be sudden in which case the local council will normally ensure that arrangements are made to secure the safety of all the home's residents.

❝ You can ask for a re-assessment if you feel your relative's needs have increased. ❞

 Information about NHS Nursing Care Contribution and NHS Continuing Healthcare is given on page 91.

Funding a care home

Moving a loved one into a care home is very difficult and emotional at the best of times and having to think about the finances and practicalities of funding a care home place is the last thing you might want to do, but it is essential that you and your relative understand the constraints that money can have on his or her right of choice, future security and comfort.

Who pays for what?

Rather like hotels, the cost of a place in a care home can vary tremendously, depending on location, quality of care home, size of room or the type of care that is needed.

The choice of care home may be dictated by cost, either because the local council will only fund up to a certain amount or, if as a relative you are prepared to top up the local council rate, you may be limited by how much you can afford. If your relative is self-funding his or her care home place, there might be a limit as to how much can practically be afforded over the long term (see the table, below, which shows average fees for care homes across the UK).

Average fees for care homes (2007/08)

	Nursing care		Residential care	
	Weekly fee (£s)	Yearly cost (£s)*	Weekly fee (£s)	Yearly cost (£s)*
North	488	25,376	394	20,488
Yorkshire & Humberside	521	27,092	409	21,268
North West	558	29,016	402	20,904
West Midlands	605	31,460	413	21,476
East Midlands	588	30,576	417	21,684
East Anglia	577	30,004	449	23,348
Northern Home Counties	815	42,380	538	27,976
Greater London	740	38,480	514	26,728
Southern Home Counties	742	38,584	482	25,064
South West	658	34,216	455	23,660
England	648	33,696	449	23,348
Wales	537	27,924	373	19,396
Scotland	557	28,964	516	26,832
Northern Ireland & Isle of Man	517	26,884	396	20,592
UK	627	32,604	445	23,140

* The average annual cost is calculated from the weekly cost assuming a 52-week year

Funding your care

Care home funding can take one of two routes depending on how much capital your relative has. This chart shows the steps to take if he or she ends up being funded wholly or partly by the local council (see also pages 168–70) or needs to fund his or her care privately (see also pages 185–90).

Does your relative have capital or savings in excess of £22,250?

Capital includes the value of your relative's former home unless it is occupied by his or her partner, a relative who is aged over 60 or is incapacitated or a child under 16 who your relative, or a former partner, who is a lone parent, is liable to maintain (aee pages 166–8). (Scotland: £21,500; Wales: £22,000; NI: £22,250.)

YES

NO

Obtain an assessment of your relative's care needs from social services.

Arrange an assessment of your relative's care needs with social services (see pages 38–48).

The local authority can help with the first 12 weeks of care costs if, apart from your relative's property, his or her other savings are below £22,250. Any help beyond this period will be through a deferred payments agreement (see pages 188–90). (Scotland: £21,500; Wales: £22,000; NI: £22,250.)

The local authority should assist with your relative's care costs. He or she would normally be expected to contribute all income less £21.15 retained for personal expenses (see page 167). (Wales: £21.38.)

Depending on your relative's other capital and income, he or she may also be able to claim Income Support or Pension Credit (see page 30).

Your relative will also have to contribute £1 per week for each £250 of capital he or she has between £13,500 and £22,250 (see page 166). (Scotland: £13,000/£21,500; Wales: £19,000/£22,000.)

Claim Attendance Allowance (see page 31). (Not payable in Scotland if a personal care contribution is being paid towards the care home fees.)

You or your relative should be able to choose which care home is preferred subject to it meeting your relative's assessed needs and being within the price that the social services are prepared to pay (see pages 168–9).

If your relative is moving into a care home providing nursing care, he or she can claim the NHS Nursing Care Contribution, which is paid direct to the home (see page 180).

If your relative wishes to live in more expensive accommodation, a third party needs to top-up the local authority funding. Your relative is not allowed to do this from capital below £22,250. (Scotland: £21,500; Wales: £22,000.)

Make sure that your relative can afford his or her chosen care over the long term. Seek advice and keep your relative's funding situation under review as circumstances change.

MEANS TESTING

If your relative has been assessed by his or her local council as needing to live in a care home (see pages 38–48), in order to qualify for local council funding towards the cost, he or she will have to undergo a means test. This means test (or financial assessment) is carried out in accordance with a set of rules that all local councils must adhere to and is contained in guidance issued to them by the Government called the 'Charging for Residential Accommodation Guide' (CRAG).

The means test is carried out by the local social services department and is based on your relative's capital and income. There are slight variations of some figures between England, Wales, Scotland and Northern Ireland (see the table opposite top), but in principle they all follow the same charging rules. The means test is carried out immediately after your relative is assessed as needing care. It will also be kept under review to take account of reductions or increases in capital and/or income over time.

Capital

Capital is the combination of your relative's savings and assets, including the value of his or her former home unless it is disregarded because of various criteria explained on page 187.

- If your relative's capital is below the **upper band (see the table, opposite top):** he or she is entitled to financial support from the local council.
- If your relative's capital is below the **lower band:** he or she is entitled to maximum support, although still having to contribute his or her income (see the Case Study, opposite bottom) less the amount he or she is allowed to retain for personal expenses.
- If your relative's capital falls between **the upper and lower bands:** he or she also has to pay a capital tariff calculated as £1 per week for each £250 or part thereof of capital they have between these two figures.

Income

Each local council sets a 'standard rate' for what they are prepared to pay for care home placements and then, if the individual has capital below that rate (as outlined left), your relative will be expected to contribute his or her income towards the cost.

The treatment of income is too complex to go into detail here as certain income can be either partially or totally disregarded. In general, however, most forms of income are fully counted and taken into account when the local council carries out its means test. Exactly what income should be fully or partially

 To read the 'Charging for residential accommodation guide' (CRAG), download it from the Department of Health website: www.dh.gov.uk.

Capital bands and personal expenses allowances in the UK

Local council funding for care home placements is available to people with limited capital and income. This table shows the upper and lower bands for the UK and the weekly amount a person is allowed to retain from his or her income to cover personal expenses. The personal expense allowance is intended to cover personal expenses only and cannot be used, for example, to pay for more expensive accommodation.

England	Lower	£13,500.00
	Upper	£22,250.00
	Personal expense allowance	£21.15
Scotland	Lower	£13,000.00
	Upper	£21,500.00
	Personal expense allowance	£21.15
Wales	Lower	£19,000.00
	Upper	£22,000.00
	Personal expense allowance	£21.38
Northern Ireland	Lower	£13,500.00
	Upper	£22,250.00
	Personal expense allowance	£21.15

Case Study   Mrs Smith

Mrs Smith is 82 years old, lives in Manchester and has been assessed as needing a care home place costing £400 per week. She has savings of £15,000 and a Pension Credit of £124.05 per week.

	Income (£s)	Expenditure (£s)
Care home fees		400.00
Pension and Pension Credit	124.05	
Tariff income £1 for each £250 between £13,500 and £22,250	3.00	
Total assumed income	127.05	
Less personal expenses allowance	21.15	
Mrs Smith's contribution		105.90
Balance paid by the local council		294.10

disregarded is listed in CRAG, which can be downloaded from the Department of Health's website (see page 166). Your relative would be expected to claim any benefits he or she is entitled to and contribute these towards the care home fees along with other income, less the amount in the table on page 167 they must retain for personal expenses.

CARE HOME CHOICES AND FUNDING

Most local councils have limited resources so you may find that when it comes to choosing your relative's care home, his or her choice will be very much restricted by cost unless you or another third party can afford to top up the local council's standard rate. Note, however, that local councils are not allowed to set an arbitrary rate for what they are prepared to pay for a care home place if care cannot be purchased in their area for that amount.

In order to purchase care at their standard rate, you may find that the local council has 'block purchased' a number of beds with some local care

> **!** Care homes that accommodate older people at the council rate sometimes charge self-funding people considerably more to subsidise the non-market rate being collected for council-funded residents.

homes. This does not mean your relative is restricted to those homes. There are rules relating to choice (see Choosing a care home on page 154), which the local councils must adhere to and these are contained in the National Assistance Act 1948 (choice of accommodation) Directions 1992. The rules relating to choice are contained within local council circular LAC(2004)20, which can be downloaded from www.dh.gov.uk.

Local council responsibilities

The local council in which your relative is deemed to be resident is responsible for the arrangement of their care home, even if he or she were to choose one in a different area.

- **If the care home chosen for your relative is more expensive** than the local council would normally pay for, that accommodation can still be chosen if a third party is willing and able to pay the extra cost. If your relative is funded by the local council, he or she is not allowed to top up the standard rate – it can only come from a third party. The exception to this rule is if your relative is receiving temporary funding through a 12-weeks property disregard or deferred payments agreement period – see pages 187–90.
- **If your relative's assessed needs cannot be met from what's on offer,** the local authority has the discretion to be able to increase its standard rate to enable those needs to be met. The

same would apply if there were no vacancies in the care homes that accept the local council rate although, if your relative was then funded by the authority in a more expensive home, the authority could reserve the right to move your relative to cheaper accommodation if a vacancy materialised at a later date.

- **If the local council offers your relative more expensive accommodation** because that is the only way they can meet his or her assessed needs, they then cannot ask for a third-party top up. In practice, however, because there are so few care homes that accept residents at the rate local councils are prepared to pay, it has become quite commonplace for them to require a third party to top up the fees when accommodating local council-funded residents.

- **If the council has agreed to contribute towards your relative's fees in a care home, your relative should be able to move to a different area.** If the move is to a more expensive area, for instance to be near family or close friends, it is important that this need is noted at your relative's assessment and written in his or her care plan. If this is done, the council should consider increasing their funding to the amount the council in the new area pays for the places it funds. If the move to a more expensive area is your relative's choice, rather than a need, the council is likely to ask for a top up to cover the increased fees.

 If you are considering the affordability of topping up your relative's funding, it is important to realise that when the care home imposes a fee increase, normally annually, the local council may not increase its standard rate by the same rate. Consequently the third-party top up could become disproportionately more, making it less affordable. See chapter 4 for help from charities and benevolent funds.

Third-party top ups

In order for your relative to be able to use a top up from a third party, he or she will need to demonstrate that the third party is able and willing to pay the difference between the local council's usual standard rate and the care home's actual fees.

The local council will need to satisfy itself that the third party has the resources to sustain such an arrangement for the likely duration and, once doing so, will enter into a formal arrangement to facilitate it. Any third-party top-up agreement should be between the council and the third party.

Case Study Mrs Jones

Mrs Jones was 78 and lived in a council flat in Wales; her daughters Pauline and Jean and their families both lived in Surrey and visited as often as they could. Mrs Jones was confused and agitated and her memory was very poor. For several years she had been receiving services from the social services department to help her stay at home. However, her confusion was getting worse, she had had two small fires in her flat and regularly knocked on her neighbours' doors in a distressed state asking why her daughter had not come home. Then one evening she went out to look for her daughters and was found 24 hours later on the local allotment.

Pauline contacted social services, asked them to reassess her mother and was with her mother when the assessment was carried out. The care manager assessed Mrs Jones as needing a care home and Pauline asked them to arrange a home in Surrey to meet her mother's social and emotional needs to be near her family. This was agreed at the assessment. Social services then sought an emergency admission to a local home for the safety of Mrs Jones and her neighbours.

Pauline contacted the care manager who said the local council would not pay for a home in Surrey. Pauline asked for a copy of the care plan and found there was no mention of Mrs Jones's need to be near her family. Pauline contacted the care manager's team leader and then a service manager who told her that the local council could not afford to pay the extra cost for a home in Surrey. Pauline made an official complaint and the matter was passed to a senior manager to investigate. The investigation upheld Pauline's complaint and found that the initial notes of the assessment had recorded Mrs Jones's need to be near her family but a lack of money meant that the council had not agreed to pay for a home in Surrey. Mrs Jones was subsequently moved to a home near her daughters.

PAYING FEES

Once the care home has been chosen and the contract agreed with the local authority, arrangements will be made for your relative to make his or her contribution towards the fees. This can be collected in two different ways:

- **The preferred arrangement is through the local council.** The council pays the

full fees to the care home and invoices your relative for his or her assessed contribution and, if appropriate, any third party for their contribution.

If the local council are making the arrangements for your relative's care home placement and you or your relative choose more expensive accommodation that will require a top up, the council is still responsible for the full cost of that accommodation. Therefore, if the local council were to place your relative in more expensive accommodation, it must contract to pay the care home's fees in full. The third-party top up to meet the cost above what the local council would normally pay will then be treated as part of your relative's income for charging purposes and collected by the council so they can recover the additional cost.

- **The council may pay just their contribution to the care home** (as long as your relative, the care home and the council agree), and the care home will then invoice your relative for his or her contribution and collect any top up direct from the third party. This route is not generally recommended because, being an individual arrangement it is outside the control of the local council contract or influence, which may help in curtailing fee increases.

NHS funding

If your relative is in a care home with nursing and receives the Nursing Care Contribution (see page 180), this will be paid directly by the NHS to the care home and will reduce the amount the council pays. Your relative will then be invoiced for his or her assessed contribution.

If your relative is in a nursing home and paying his or her own fees, the nursing care contribution will still be paid directly by the NHS to the nursing home. The home will then deduct this amount from your relative's fees.

COUPLES

What was once a financially comfortable retirement can be devastated when one member of a couple needs to move into a care home. Even if the local council is helping with the cost, if it's the member of a couple who receives most of the family income moving into a care home, it can leave the partner at home with very little income. If your relative is moving into a care home and is leaving a partner at home, or it may be that both of them require care, it's important to understand how their income and capital is treated by the local council in the means test for financial support.

One member of a couple requiring care

The local council can only financially assess the member of a couple who requires the care home place. In doing so, they will take into account:

- **Savings and capital** in their name and 50 per cent of any jointly held capital.
- **All that person's income,** less the amount he or she is allowed to retain for personal expenses (£21.15 per week, £21.38 in Wales). However, the local council does have the discretion to increase this amount for the benefit of the partner remaining at home if he or she is experiencing severe financial hardship.
- **In the case of married couples or civil partnerships,** 50 per cent of any private pension can be ignored and returned to the partner remaining at home.

Where the person in the care home is the main recipient of an unmarried couples' overall income, such as an occupational pension, the local council can use discretion to increase the personal expenses allowance in special circumstances to enable them to pass some of that income to the partner remaining at home. Depending on their capital and income the partner remaining at home may be able to claim Pension Credit or other means-tested benefits in their own right (see pages 30–6).

Another anomaly between married and unmarried couples (and that includes civil partnerships) is that Sections 42 and 43 of the National Assistance Act 1948, known as the liable relative's rule, states that married couples are liable to maintain each other and this can include contributing towards the cost of care home fees if one member of the couple is being accommodated at the expense of the local council. However, because this provision is now widely regarded as anachronistic, the Government has announced its intention to repeal it.

Making joint savings work efficiently

Where savings are held jointly, the local council will only take into account the 50 per cent share of those savings as belonging to the person needing care. Because of this, it could be advantageous to separate joint savings into two separate accounts, allowing the care costs to be paid just from the account of the person in the care home. The effect of this is that only the savings belonging to the member of the couple that needs care are depleted and the means test capital limit, where the local council will assist with the funding, is reached earlier. This is illustrated below and can be done at any time.

	One account	Two separate accounts	
	Joint account (£s)	Partner in care (£s: 50%)	Partner at home (£s: 50%)
Account balance	60,000	30,000	30,000
Savings used to pay care fees before capital limit reached	15,500	7,750	–
Leaving for means test	**44,500**	**22,250**	**30,000**
	x 50% = 22,250 means test limit. Eligibility to state funding after £15,500 paid in care fees	Fees paid only by the partner in care. Eligibility to state assistance after £7,750 paid (saving of £7,750)	

The removal of the rule will require a change to primary legislation and the Department of Health is seeking an appropriate legislative vehicle at the earliest possible opportunity. In the meantime, local councils have been provided with extra money to enable them to exercise their discretion to **not** apply the rule. In Scotland, a Bill to abolish liable relative rules is currently going through parliament.

Both members of a couple requiring care

If both members of a couple are assessed as needing care, the local council must carry out separate means tests according to their own or jointly owned resources. It has no power to assess a couple according to their combined resources. Different rules may apply in respect of entitlement to Pension Credit if it is considered that both members living in the same care home constitutes being members of the same household. This may depend on whether they share the same room or live in separate rooms or wings of the care home. In the latter circumstance, the Department of Work and Pensions should certainly assess them separately.

❝ The local council cannot assess a couple according to their combined resources. ❞

TREATMENT OF TRUSTS

Your relative might be a beneficiary of a trust fund, which could hold money or property for his or her benefit. The terms of the trust, the details of the beneficiaries and the trustee(s) who administer it would normally be contained within a trust deed or it could be in the form of a will or deed of settlement. If your relative has an interest in a trust, it could be either in the form of an absolute entitlement to capital or income from the trust, or entitlement to capital or income at the discretion of the trustees.

- **If your relative has an absolute entitlement to the capital in a trust,** the local council will treat him or her as if he or she possessed that capital. It might be that your relative is not the only beneficiary of the trust and has a shared interest in the capital. In these circumstances, the local council would divide the value equally between the beneficiaries and treat your relative as owning an equal share.
- **If your relative's entitlement is to the income of the trust,** similarly the local council will treat that entitlement as income and count it in the means test for funding.
- **If, however, your relative were entitled to both the capital and income of a trust,** then he or she would be treated as possessing the capital, as above, but the income would not be counted in the income assessment.

Discretionary trust Where money or assets are held in trust and payments from the trust are made wholly at the discretion of the trustees and there is no absolute entitlement either to capital or income

If the trust is a **discretionary trust** and your relative has no absolute entitlement either to capital or income, the local council should only take into account the actual payments that are made wholly at the discretion of the trustees.

THE HOME

Over 70 per cent of people aged over 65 own their own homes and, according to research by the Liberal Democrats, over 70,000 homes are sold each year to pay for care. However, your relative need not necessarily have to do this.

If your relative owns his or her own home it will be disregarded from the means test if the stay in a care home is considered to be temporary and your relative intends to return home.

If, however, the move to a care home is permanent, the value of the property will be disregarded for a period of 12 weeks if your relative's other capital is below the higher means-test threshold and his or her income is insufficient to meet the care costs. This is called the 12-weeks property disregard. The only circumstances in which your relative's property could be totally disregarded are where it is occupied by:

- **Your relative's former partner** (who is not estranged or divorced from your relative).
- **A relative who is aged over 60** or is incapacitated. (Incapacitated is defined as being entitled to Incapacity Benefit, Severe Disablement Allowance, Disability Living Allowance, Attendance Allowance,

! If your relative moves into a care home and his or her property is left empty, then he or she should receive full exemption from council tax until it is sold.

❝❝ Over 70 per cent of people aged over 65 own their own homes and more than 70,000 homes are sold each year to pay for care. ❞❞

The 12-weeks property disregard is explained on page 187. This is a form of support that may be available to your relative if he or she has been assessed as needing permanent residence in a care home.

Selling-up

Should your relative's partner remain at home and he or she decides to sell the property and move into smaller, less expensive accommodation, as often can be the case, his or her 50 per cent share of the proceeds could be taken into account in your relative's means test. However, although living in a care home, your relative could well wish to make available part of his or her share of the proceeds to the partner at home to enable the purchase of the smaller property. In these circumstances, the local council guidance states that it would be reasonable for this amount to be disregarded, leaving only the surplus of the partner's share to be taken into account.

Constant Attendance Allowance (see pages 34–5), or an analogous benefit whether claimed or not.)

- A child under the age of 16 years who your relative is liable to maintain.
- A lone parent who is your relative's estranged or divorced partner.

The local council also has the discretion to ignore the property in special circumstances, for example, if it is the sole residence of someone who previously cared for your relative and gave up his or her own home to be able to do this. If the local council were to allow this discretion, the property would be taken into account later if the carer were to die

or move out. The benefits agency does not have this discretion for Pension Credit.

Legal versus beneficial ownership

The treatment of your relative's property and whether its value will be counted in the means test will depend on whether he or she is the legal or beneficial owner. In most circumstances people are both, but sometimes the legal owner – the person in whose name the property is registered – can be different from the beneficial owner, being the person entitled to the proceeds of property should it be sold.

This circumstance could arise, for example, where children have put up the money to buy their parents' council house with the intention of eventually profiting from the investment. In such circumstance, the parents would need to negotiate with the local council to establish the true position. It may be, for example, that the local council would argue that the value of the discount given when the property was purchased equates to their beneficial interest and that the remainder of the value can be disregarded.

The same 'horse dealing' may be necessary where children have spent large sums of money improving their

❝ Sometimes the legal owner is different from the beneficial owner, for example, where children have bought their parents' house. ❞

parents' property with the intention of being repaid on its eventual sale. It can also be the case that the issues around jointly owned property discussed on page 176 come into play if a parent sells their home and uses the proceeds to jointly purchase a larger property with their children to accommodate both them and their children's family.

Joint tenants versus tenants in common

If one member of a couple moves into a care home, the value of his or her property is disregarded as long as the partner continues to occupy it. If this were the scenario, it might also be worth changing the ownership of the property from **joint tenancy** to **tenants in common**. Your relative could then will his or her half of the property to beneficiaries rather than to the partner so that if your relative dies first, that half will not pass automatically to the surviving partner and get caught in the means test for care, as it would under joint tenancy. It may be necessary for your relatives to change the terms of their wills to accommodate this. Take professional legal advice before considering this action.

> **" The value of a 'share' of a property can depend on the circumstances of the joint ownership. "**

Jargon buster

Joint tenancy Joint tenants jointly own the whole property and on death of one of the joint owners their interest in it automatically passes to the other as if it were in trust for them. Most properties that are bought by couples are held as joint tenancies

Tenants in common Joint ownership of property where each joint tenant owns a separate share in the property, typically 50:50, and consequently they can will their separate share to whoever they wish

Jointly owned property

If your relative's property is jointly owned by another person who does not occupy the property or fulfil any of the above disregard conditions, the local council can take your relative's share into account. However, it's not straightforward because the value of a 'share' of a property can depend on the circumstances of the joint ownership. The value to be taken into account would be the value of your relative's interest in the property, bearing in mind his or her ability to re-assign the beneficial interest to somebody else and whether it is constrained and/or the possibility of finding a willing buyer for his or her share.

It may well be construed that because a joint owner has a right to occupy the property it is unlikely that there would be a buyer prepared to share in that right to occupy it. Consequently, the only person who may be interested in purchasing your relative's share would be the joint owner, effectively determining the 'market value' as nil. If necessary, you or your relative should seek legal advice in these circumstances.

If the jointly owned property remains unsold, the local council cannot place a charge against it as they can to recover monies laid out on behalf of someone utilising the deferred payments scheme. They can, however, register a similar but less effective caution against the property, which would alert them when the property was in the process of being sold or transferred.

Pension Credit

The rules for Pension Credit follow a Commissioner's decision CIS/ 15936/1996, where it was held that the valuation of jointly owned property should be based on the actual market value of the claimant's share and this value may depend on whether there would be a willing buyer of the claimant's interest in the property.

Disputing the valuation

If there is a disparity between how the local council and the benefits agency value the property, resulting in your relative not being entitled to the Pension Credit element of their income contributing towards the local council's assessed charge, the amount to be paid by the local council should be that much more.

Where the local council is unsure about your relative's share or their valuation is disputed by your relative or his or her representative, seek a professional valuation. The name on the deeds of the property should establish ownership and, in normal circumstances, joint owners have equal shares. However, if ownership is disputed and your relative's interest is alleged to be less than seems apparent from initial information, the local council will require written evidence on any beneficial interest they or the other joint owners possess.

Information about deferred payment agreements is given on pages 188–90.

Gifting assets

It is quite likely that your relative will see his or her property as the main asset that has been worked and saved for. The thought of having to use its value to pay for care when others who were perhaps less prudent receive free care from the state may feel so inequitable that your relative will consider giving it away just in case care becomes necessary.

In fact, the desire to give away assets is now such a common consideration that an industry has built up offering trusts and other products to hive off assets out of the reach of local councils. But it is not that simple.

LEGAL TRANSFER OF PROPERTY

If your relative is assessed as needing to live in a care home, during the means test the local council will ask if he or she owns or ever owned a property. If the answer to the latter is yes but your relative no longer owns the property, the local council will investigate to ascertain under what circumstances the property was disposed of.

If it were then considered that your relative disposed of or gifted the property to avoid paying for care, the local council can treat your relative as if he or she still owned it. This is referred to as 'notional

capital' and through the provisions of the Health and Social Security Adjudication Act 1983 (HASSASSA), funding from the local council would not be forthcoming until that notional capital would have depleted to the means test limit. If the transfer took place within six months of being assessed by the local council as needing care and admission to a care home provided under Part III of the National Assistance Act, the liability for the assessed charge can be recovered from the third party that received the asset.

The same consideration is given to all assets. If the local council considers that your relative has deliberately deprived him- or herself of a capital asset that would otherwise be counted in a means test, they would carefully look at the reason for disposing of it.

Of course, avoiding the means test for care may not be your relative's main

 For more information about gifting assets, see the *Which? Essential Guide* to *Wills and Probate*.

motive for disposing of an asset, and in order for it to be considered as deprivation, it must be a significant one. There is no time limit as to how far back a local council can go in considering whether someone has deprived him- or herself of capital. However, if the transfer took place at a time when your relative was fit and healthy and could not have foreseen a need for a move to a care home, there may have genuinely been other reasons for transferring the asset rather than that of deliberate deprivation.

BE CAREFUL!

What could go wrong when giving away assets? It is important for your relative to remember that circumstances and relationships can change, which could have serious implications, particularly relating to his or her home. For example, if your relative were to give away his or her property without retaining the right to occupy it for the remainder of his or her life, or with the retained right to sell it and purchase more suitable property as needs change, he or she could be left in a very vulnerable position. Consider, for example, if the person to whom the property was transferred became bankrupt, or divorced and the value of the property was divided up in a divorce court. Alternatively, the recipient of the property could borrow against it and,

as a result, any net sale proceeds in the future could be inadequate to purchase more suitable retirement housing or if they defaulted on a loan a sale might be forced.

The security of owning your own property and the freedom of choice with that ownership is a lot to sacrifice, particularly if you consider that if your relative did deprive him- or herself of assets (and got away with it), his or her choice of care home could very much be restricted by the funding provided by the local council. This may not be what your relative would otherwise choose if he or she had the means to do so. Similarly, giving away money or other assets may be at the cost of the financial security your relative needs to provide, without worry, a well-deserved comfortable life style in retirement.

❝Remember that circumstances and relationships can change, with serious implications for all parties. ❞

NHS funding for care homes

The NHS is responsible for providing nursing care to people who need it and in October 2001 the Government decided that it wasn't fair that people receiving nursing care in care homes had to pay for it, so they introduced a scheme where the NHS makes a contribution towards this cost.

In principle, NHS nursing care can be delivered in any setting including, in some cases, being part of a complete care package of fully funded NHS Continuing Healthcare. Guidance covering the assessment process and eligibility to NHS Continuing Healthcare in England is contained in a National Framework for NHS Continuing Healthcare published on 1 October 2007. The framework for this assessment process is discussed below.

❝ The NHS contributes even for short stays. ❞

The amount of the contribution

The weekly amount of the contribution varies between England, Wales and Northern Ireland. England's contribution is £101 per week, Wales is £117.66 and Northern Ireland is £100. In Scotland, your relative would receive £147 per week as a contribution towards personal care and an additional £67 per week for nursing care. These contributions should be reflected in the fees charged by the home to your relative.

Intermediate care

Intermediate care in a care home can be provided to your relative free of charge (see page 70).

NHS Nursing Care Contribution

If your relative is assessed as needing to live in a care home that provides nursing care, he or she should have also undergone an assessment to ascertain eligibility for fully funded NHS Continuing Healthcare (see page 182), which would meet the full cost. Failing this, your relative should be eligible for an NHS Nursing Care Contribution.

All residents of care homes that provide nursing, whether they are self-funding or local council funded, should undergo an assessment to confirm their need for input from a registered nurse to meet their care needs. If applicable, a non-means-tested contribution is paid by the NHS direct to the nursing home towards the weekly fees.

Even if your relative's stay in the nursing home is temporary, he or she should be entitled to the NHS Nursing Care Contribution and, if it is for a period of less than six weeks, then an assessment for the contribution does not have to take place; the NHS contribution can be paid based on information obtained from the nursing home or GP. This is particularly worth noting if your relative requires regular short periods of respite care.

The contribution towards your relative's nursing care if the care home is in England, Wales or Scotland will not affect his or her benefits. For example, if your relative is receiving Attendance Allowance, he or she will continue to do so. If the care home is in Scotland and your relative is receiving the contribution towards his or her personal and nursing care, he or she will cease to be eligible for attendance allowance. If your relative needed hospitalisation, his or her contribution from the NHS will stop, although the care home may require that the full weekly fees continue to be paid to retain the room.

Following an initial assessment for NHS Nursing Care Contribution, if this reveals your relative is not entitled to NHS Continuing Healthcare, a review of eligibility should be undertaken within three months and then annually or more frequently if there is a significant change in your relative's nursing needs. As a matter of course, potential eligibility for NHS Continuing Healthcare should always be checked during the review. To

Other NHS services

Other services available to your relative from the NHS, regardless of the type of care home he or she is living in, include:

- A needs assessment for continence aids paid for by the NHS.
- Specialist NHS support (as available), such as chiropody, physiotherapy or equipment including pressure relief mattresses and mobility or communication aids.

The responsible Primary Care Trust (PCT) is that in which the GP practice where your relative is registered resides. The PCT can be contacted through your relative's GP or care home manager.

ascertain this, the NHS uses a checklist of criteria that may lead to a full assessment for NHS Continuing Healthcare as explained on page 182.

It is important to realise that many of the conditions requiring older people to move into nursing homes can lead to considerable deterioration of health and if this were the case with your relative, remember a review for NHS Continuing Healthcare funding can be requested at any time through the nursing home.

If you disagree with an NHS assessment and wish to dispute it, go to page 204 where there is information on the NHS complaints procedure.

NHS Continuing Healthcare

NHS Continuing Healthcare can include the full cost of a place in a nursing home, but there is a very fine line between what is considered to be free healthcare provided by the NHS and means-tested social care, which is the responsibility of local councils. To assist in deciding which treatment and other health services it is appropriate for the NHS to provide, the Secretary of State has developed the concept of 'a primary health need'. Where a person's primary need is a 'health need', the NHS is regarded as responsible for providing for all their needs in any setting.

The assessment is conducted by NHS health practitioners whose experience and professional judgement should enable them to make a decision about your relative's eligibility for NHS Continuing Healthcare. The assessment should be multi-disciplinary, include your relative's and relevant family involvement, be based on your relative's needs not on his or her location and be independent of budgetary constraints the PCT may be incurring.

The decision as to whether your relative is eligible for NHS Continuing Healthcare is two-fold:

- **Making an assessment that looks at all your relative's relevant needs.** This assessment is conducted in accordance with the National Framework for Continuing Healthcare used by all PCTs in partnership with their local councils. It sets out the principles and processes for establishing primary health need and eligibility to NHS Continuing Healthcare. The assessment uses a checklist to identify people who are most likely to be eligible for NHS Continuing Healthcare and who should be referred for full consideration and assessment.

- **If it is decided that your relative should be referred, a decision support tool (see opposite) is then used**. This ensures that the full range of factors that have a bearing on eligibility are taken into account in making a decision on whether NHS Continuing Healthcare is needed.

If the assessment reveals that your relative has priority needs in one of the four priority care domains or severe levels of need in two or more domains,

❝ Where someone's primary need is a 'health need', the NHS must provide for all their needs in any setting. ❞

For more information about NHS Continuing Healthcare in England, go to
www.dh.gov.uk/en/SocialCare/Deliveringadultsocialcare/Continuingcare/index.htm.

The decision support tool

The decision support tool covers 11 areas called 'care domains', which are:

- Behaviour
- Cognition
- Psychological and emotional
- Communication
- Mobility
- Nutrition
- Continence
- Skin and tissue viability
- Breathing
- Drug therapies and medication: symptom control
- Altered states of consciousness

Through assessment, these are measured and your relative would be defined as having a low, moderate, high or severe level of need in each domain or, in the case of behaviour, breathing, drug therapies (symptom control) and altered states of consciousness, whether they also have a priority level of need.

" A number of domains with high and/or moderate needs can indicate a primary health need. "

If your relative has a rapidly deteriorating condition that may be entering a terminal phase, he or she could need urgent consideration as to eligibility for **NHS Continuing Healthcare**. If this were the case, your relative would not have to go through the normal assessment process but could be found to be eligible using a special fast-track pathway tool.

then it is likely that he or she would be eligible for NHS Continuing Healthcare.

If there are a number of domains with high and/or moderate needs, this can also indicate a primary health need. In this case, the overall need, the interactions between needs in different care domains, and the evidence from risk assessments, should be taken into account in deciding whether or not to recommend eligibility to NHS Continuing Healthcare.

183

Qualifying for NHS Continuing Healthcare

If your relative were to qualify, the NHS would contract and pay the care home direct. Your relative will not have the right to choose either the location (town) or the actual nursing home to which he or she will move. However, government guidance has reminded Primary Care Trusts (PCTs) that assessments and decision-making should be person-centred and your relative should be enabled to participate in informed decisions about his or her future care including the choice of nursing homes that are able to meet their assessed needs within the criteria set by the PCT.

If following assessment your relative's needs in all domains are recorded as 'low' or 'no need', this would indicate ineligibility to NHS Continuing Healthcare and any state funding will be subject to means-testing through the local council (see pages 166–7). The majority of older people in care homes do not meet the criteria for NHS funding. Currently only around 30,000 people are in receipt of Continuing Healthcare packages from the NHS.

❝ Your relative should be enabled to take part in informed decisions about his or her future care, including choice of nursing home. ❞

NHS Continuing Healthcare in Wales, Scotland and Northern Ireland

- In Wales, local health boards are responsible for local health services and many of the rules that apply in England also apply in Wales, although there are some differences. At the time of writing, a draft national framework for NHS Continuing Healthcare is going through a consultation process. It is proposed to use a decision support tool similar to that used in England.
- In Scotland, the assessment for NHS Continuing Healthcare is made under the Single Shared Assessment Approach and the decision based on whether a person's current needs are primarily 'health' needs. The Scottish Executive is planning to develop and pilot an additional assessment tool to promote consistency across Scotland.
- In Northern Ireland, there is no guidance on NHS-funded Healthcare.

To find out more about Continuing Healthcare in Wales, see Circular NAFWC 41/2004 on http://new.wales.gov.uk/publications/circular/circulars04 and click on the Welsh or English tab. For Scotland, go to www.sehd.scot.nhs.uk/mels/cel2008_06.pdf.

Private funding

In no other walk of life would you consider realising an asset worth what could be hundreds of thousands of pounds and pay annual bills of anything from £20,000 to £50,000 a year without seeking advice. Yet many people each year consider doing so to fund their care costs.

The reason for this anomaly might be a pure lack of awareness that specialist financial advice is available or it may be that relatives find the whole situation just too traumatic and complacently accept their relative's situation as a fait accompli. Whatever the reason, many families have learnt at great expense that failing to seek appropriate advice at the right time has cost their relatives large amounts of money and in some circumstances placed them in very precarious situations with care homes.

GETTING ADVICE

The importance of seeking specialist financial advice cannot be overstated and is something the Financial Services Authority (FSA) has recognised by introducing the requirement that financial advisers wishing to advise on funding long-term care must first attain a specialist qualification called 'CF8'. To obtain this qualification, financial advisers must sit a special examination to test their understanding of local council charging and assessment procedures, what the NHS must provide, eligibility to benefits from the Department of Work and Pensions and the legal issues surrounding attorneys or

receivers handling other people's money. The advantages gained by seeking professional advice are many:

- **It can be a health check** to ensure your relative is claiming everything they are entitled to from the various state pots and provide you or your relative with an understanding of what financial products are available to assist in mitigating what can be very high care costs.
- **It gives you and your relative the ability to assess the affordability** of his or her chosen care over the medium and long terms.

> ❝ Many families have learnt at great expense about the value of seeking appropriate advice. ❞

LONG-TERM MONEY CONCERNS

One of the most common problems older people and their relatives face is what happens if the money runs out. If your relative's capital reduces to the means-test threshold (see page 166), he or she will need to seek local council assistance with the care funding. In these circumstances you may find that the home costs more than the local council usually pays and, if it won't reduce its fees to the local council rate, your relative may have to find a source of top up or seek less expensive accommodation. However, moving care homes could be detrimental to his or her health and wellbeing and should be avoided unless it is absolutely necessary.

 Care homes often charge self-funders more than they charge residents for whom the local council pays. If your relative is self-funding, he or she can ask the council to make the contract with the care home on his or her behalf, but the care home may be unwilling to accept your relative at the council rate if they are aware he or she is paying the full fees.

❝ If your relative qualifies, the local council will disregard the value of their property for 12 weeks. ❞

MOVING TOWARDS PRIVATE FUNDING

To avoid the precarious situation described above, it is essential that your relative:

- **Receives a needs assessment** from the local council right at the outset (see pages 38–48) so that you know you are choosing a care home that matches those assessed needs.
- **Gets professional financial advice** so he or she can look at the finances and work out whether the fees the home are charging are affordable from the capital and income your relative has at his or her disposal. If not, your relative should raise the matter with the care home straightaway to ascertain if they would continue to accommodate him or her at the local council rate and,

if not, what sort of top up would be required and where would it come from?
- Checks if some funding and support might still be available to him or her, including the non-means-tested Attendance Allowance (see page 34) and the NHS Nursing Care Contribution (see page 180).

HOW TO GET FINANCIAL HELP WITHOUT SELLING PROPERTY

Once it has been determined that your relative's property will be treated as capital and, assuming its value is greater than the means-test limit, there is some financial assistance available if your relative does not wish to or cannot sell the property immediately and fit the qualifying criteria. This financial support is from the local council in the form of the 12-weeks property disregard and the deferred payments scheme.

12-weeks property disregard

This form of support is available to your relative if he or she has been assessed as needing a permanent residence in a care home. If your relative qualifies, the local council will disregard the value of the property for the first 12 weeks of living in the care home and assist with the funding up to the amount the council would normally pay for a care home place for someone with your relative's assessed needs.

As described in the means test (see page 166), your relative will have to contribute his or her assessed income less £21.15 (£21.38 in Wales) retained for personal expenses towards the care home fees from the date of being assessed as requiring permanent residential care for a period of 12 weeks, or until the property sells, if sooner.

To be eligible for this funding your relative must:

- Be assessed as needing permanent residential accommodation, which can be accommodation provided by either a local council or a private or voluntary care home.
- Have other capital apart from the value of the property that is below the upper means test threshold (see page 166).
- Have adequate income to meet the full cost of his or her care.

The 12-weeks property disregard is mandatory and local councils are under a statutory obligation to apply it once they

 It is important your relative receives a needs assessment (see pages 38–48) to confirm he or she requires a care home placement to qualify for this funding. Do not allow your relative to be discharged from hospital or to move from home and just be given a list of care homes.

are aware of a care home resident to whom it applies. If the local council delays the provision of this funding, it would not affect your relative's entitlement to it. Therefore, if it was subsequently discovered that your relative missed out on this funding, the local council would be liable to reimburse your relative if he or she consequently paid a higher contribution towards the care costs than was necessary during this mandatory disregard period. To make sure your relative does not miss out on this funding, you should arrange a needs assessment by the local council.

Attendance Allowance

If your relative receives Attendance Allowance, because the local council are assisting with the funding of his or her care during the 12-weeks property disregard period, the allowance will be withdrawn after the fourth week of funding but then reinstated after the 12-week period has expired.

Deferred payments agreements

Once the 12-weeks property disregard period has passed and if your relative does not wish to or has been unable to sell their home, he or she may qualify for entering into a deferred payments agreement with the local council. The local council will then continue to provide funding towards the care home fees, as described on pages 170–1, but will require it to be repaid.

The contribution from the local council will be secured against the value of your relative's property and recovered by them from the eventual sale proceeds. The loan is interest free up until 56 days after your relative dies at which point interest will be added at a rate set by the local council at that time. This facility would be available to your relative if his or her:

- Other assets are less than the upper capital limit (see page 166).
- Income is insufficient to cover the care home fees.

Local councils have discretion over whether to operate this arrangement. For example, they may not wish to enter into an agreement with your relative if it was considered that the cost of the care he or she has chosen may not be affordable over the long term.

Taking a deferred payment could adversely affect your relative's DWP benefits. If the property is not being sold, it may be treated as capital by the DWP and, subject to the value, entitlement to

Topping up

While benefiting from the 12-weeks property disregard funding or a deferred payments arrangement, it may be necessary to top up the amount that the local council is prepared to pay. Normally, if receiving local council funding, it is not possible for someone to top up their own fees, but in these circumstances your relative would be regarded as a private payer and allowed to top up the local council contribution from disregarded income, earnings or capital with the proviso that:

- The top up during the 12-week period must not exceed the lower capital limit; in England, this is £13,500, (the equivalent of £1,125 per week) (see page 167 for figures in Wales, Scotland and Northern Ireland).
- The level of tariff income assessed (£1 for each £250 of capital between £13,500 and £22,250 in England) remains the same even though the capital may reduce as a result of topping up during the 12-week period.

Your relative can top up the local council funding during the 12-weeks property disregard and deferred payments agreement periods from his or her own resources if the local council considers it affordable.

Pension Credit could cease, leaving your relative with less income to meet the fees during this period. If, on the other hand, it is intended to sell the property and it is on the market, entitlement to

The pros and cons of accepting a deferred payments agreement

Pros

- Any growth in the property value will contribute towards the loan's repayment.
- Your relative may be able to let the property and contribute the rent towards the fees.
- The decision to sell the property can be deferred while all options for meeting the care costs are being considered.

Cons

- If the property is not on the market, it could be treated as capital and adversely affect your relative's entitlement to Pension Credit.
- The loan is only deferring a liability repayable from the eventual proceeds of the property, which will require maintaining and insuring.
- Many older people's properties are not in a condition suitable for letting and may require updating or considerable repair work to bring them up to standard.
- Letting property can often be troublesome and rental income is taxable.
- The level of local council funding available with a deferred payments agreement if at their standard rate is likely to restrict your relative's choice of care home unless a top up is affordable over the long term.
- If entering into a deferred payments agreement, the local council may also ask your relative to cover the costs of land registry searches and any other such legal costs up front.

Attendance Allowance (see page 34) and Pension Credit with the severe disability addition (see page 31) continue.

Letting the property: If it were decided to let your relative's property while entering into a deferred payments agreement, the rental income is not counted as income when working out your relative's assessed charge towards the standard rate. This is because the property is already counted as capital. Any rent you

Nursing care contributions

If your relative is moving into a care home that provides nursing and he or she is entitled to the NHS Nursing Care Contribution described on pages 180–1, this will be paid to the care home after the 12-weeks property disregard period has expired. During that period the difference between the local council's standard rate for the nursing home fees and your relative's assessed charge will be met by the local council and NHS.

The benefit of placing a property on the market

	Property **not** on the market (£s)	Property **on** the market (£s)
Weekly care home fees	400.00	400.00
Attendance Allowance	67.00	67.00
Pension/Pension Credit with severe disability addition	90.95	174.40
Personal expenses allowance	–21.15	–21.15
Income contribution towards fees	136.80	220.25
Leaving a shortfall creating a loan against the property	263.20	179.75
First 12 weeks local council funded	Nil	Nil
Total of next 14 weeks income shortfall	3,684.80	2,526.50

If it took 26 weeks to sell the property, the current saving through having the property on the market and receiving full Pension Credit can therefore be up to £1,168.30.

receive from letting it could therefore be used to top up the local council funding, which could well be less than the care home charges. It is important, however, to remember that rental income is taxable and you should allow for that and be prepared to accept that should there be a break between rental periods, an alternative source of top up might be required.

You and/or your relative would need to consider the different options for meeting the care costs and it would be prudent to seek professional advice at this stage. For example, it may well be better to sell the property and purchase an Immediate Need Care Fee Payment Plan (see page 192), which can potentially cap the cost of the care to the cost of the plan.

While such a plan can provide an income for your relative for as along as he or she needs care, investing the balance of the proceeds could also provide an additional income or the potential of capital growth for an eventual inheritance.

 For more information about letting, see the *Which? Essential Guide* to *Renting and Letting.*

Financing immediate care

Ideal financial products for meeting care home fees are those that can provide a regular income and incorporate the flexibility required to meet any future changes in care costs or circumstances, such as fee increases or the additional cost of nursing care as opposed to just personal care.

Those products that lend themselves to these criteria vary according to age, health, required income and the degree of financial risk a family is prepared to take. While interest rates remain low, leaving monies in banks or building societies is rarely a suitable option so the aim is to seek financial products that can deliver a higher income than deposits combined with the degree of certainty and safety required to sustain the cost of the care home fees for as long as care is needed.

Suitable financial products will depend on individual circumstances and your views on investment and risk. Investment bonds and/or ISAs could be one option that may provide a greater return than leaving money on deposit as well as being able to facilitate regular withdrawals. Investment bonds also have the advantage of providing an enhanced surrender value on death, normally 101 per cent of the fund value. Alternatively, specially designed Immediate Need Care Fee Payment Plans can provide the certainty of a regular income.

❝ Investment bonds and/or ISAs could provide a greater return than leaving money on deposit and money can still be withdrawn. ❞

 For more information about investment bonds and ISAs, see the *Which? Essential Guide: Save and Invest.*

IMMEDIATE NEED CARE FEE PAYMENT PLANS

These products are available only through financial advisers with the CF8 qualification. They are similar to annuities, but offer a higher level of guaranteed income for as long as care is needed and have greater tax advantages than can usually be provided by traditional investments or annuities. Furthermore, they may require only part of your relative's capital to be used to meet care costs allowing the remainder to be invested for growth and provide for an eventual inheritance if that is what your relative wishes.

These plans can provide level or increasing payments of up to 5 per cent per annum compound for as long as care is needed, covering the shortfall between income and initial care costs. The price is subject to medical underwriting and, unlike usual life or health insurance, the more impaired your relative's life, the lower the plan would cost.

While potentially capping the cost of care, these plans offer the reassurance that an increasing income towards care

The price of Immediate Need Care Fee Payment Plans

The prices of plans will vary according to individual circumstances.

Gender (M or F)	M	F	F
Date of birth	5 January 1913	23 February 1910	22 January 1920
Plan income pcm (£) increasing at 5% per annum	1,850	2,640	980
Health impairment	Heart	Stroke	Dementia and stroke
Failing activities of daily living			
Dressing	Yes	Yes	Yes
Bathing	No	Yes	Yes
Feeding	Yes	Yes	Yes
Toileting	Yes	Yes	Yes
Mobility	Yes	Yes	Yes
Cognitive	Yes	No	Yes
Company offers: income escalating at 5% per annum compound (£s)			
Company A	77,135	105,661	43,536
Company B	72,843	104,651	58,783
Company C	86,063	94,152	80,523

costs can be received as long as care is needed regardless of any changes to the economy, interest rates or stock markets. Some capital protection can be included for an extra cost, although standard plans do not normally provide for return of capital on death. The sensitivity therefore of judging whether they are suitable cannot be over estimated. You and/or your relative must consider the possible short-term loss of capital against the peace-of-mind factor that the cost of the care can potentially be capped to the cost of the plan.

" Standard plans usually do not provide for return of capital on death. "

Medical reports

Your relative would not have to undergo an intrusive medical examination as the evidence of a health and medical report is provided by his or her GP or the care home from your relative's records.

Case Study Mr Barker

Mr Barker is in hospital. He has suffered a stroke and now needs to move into a care home. Apart from a house valued at £200,000, he has £15,000 in bank and building society deposits. He is aged 80 and now needs total nursing care for the rest of his life. A care home has been chosen where the fees are £500 per week (£2,167 per month).

Income and costs per month

Item	Income (£s)	Cost (£s)
Care home fees		2,167
Money needed for personal expenses		160
Total income requirement		**2,327**
Existing income		
Basic State Pension (£90.95 per week)	394	
Attendance Allowance at higher rate (£67 per week)	290	
Occupational Pension (net of tax)	400	
Total income	1,084	
Income shortfall		**1,243**

An Immediate Need Care Fee Payment Plan providing an income of £1,243 rising by 5 per cent per annum for life, nil capital protection will take care of the initial shortfall in fees and could cost in the region of £62,000. Of the remaining capital, £20,000 could be left on deposit to cover contingencies and the balance of £133,000 could be invested primarily for growth and a potential inheritance for the family.

If such a plan is considered, it is important to ensure that your IFA approaches all insurance companies that offer them for quotes because their prices can vary tremendously depending on their actuarial interpretation of life expectancy with different conditions. For example, one company might consider Alzheimer's disease to be more life threatening than another.

The income from these plans is paid direct to the care home as a contribution towards the care fees and if paid in this way rather than to your relative, it would be tax free.

Immediate Need Care Fee Payment Plans are certainly worth considering, particularly as the insurance companies do not make any charge for quoting, even though they incur a cost for obtaining medical evidence.

It is also important to weigh all the different options for meeting the fees and comparing how your relative's capital is managing to sustain the cost, bearing in mind that fees will increase each year.

Even after deciding with your financial adviser on how best to meet the cost of your relative's care home, keep things under review as circumstances may change. For example, many long-term conditions are progressive and as health deteriorates, your relative could become eligible for funding from the NHS or be entitled to move up from lower rate to higher rate Attendance Allowance.

❝ Weigh all the options for meeting the fees, bearing in mind that costs will rise each year. ❞

Negotiating a fair contract

Before your relative moves into a care home he or she needs clear details about the services to expect and the costs. Complex funding arrangements, with contributions potentially coming from the local council, the NHS, the family or other third parties, as well as your relative, mean there could be a range of contractual relationships and scope for misunderstandings.

10

The basics

The contract is a legal document affecting your relative's future so it is important to make sure he or she is happy with it and there is nothing in it that you and they are not prepared to agree.

The terms of the contract must be fair, must take your relative's interests into account and must be intelligible to ordinary consumers without legal advice. This means using words in their normal sense and avoiding jargon, such as 'indemnity' and 'waiver of surety'. The contract must also be legible, which includes print size, colour, background and quality of paper used. You and your relative should read the contract before your relative enters the home and, if anything is unclear, ask.

WHO CONTRACTS WHO?

In most cases the legal contract for your relative's stay in a care home will be between the care home and the person or organisation that is paying the fees and other charges. This means there could be up to four contracts covering your relative's care home fees.

With the care home

All care homes in England, Wales, Scotland and Northern Ireland are required to ensure that residents moving into the home have a written contract or statement of terms and conditions setting out the services and facilities the home will provide.

" Read the contract before your relative enters the home and if anything is unclear, ask about it. "

- **If your relative is paying for his or her own care,** this will be in the form of a legal contract between your relative and the care home.
- **If the local council is contributing to your relative's funding,** the legal contract will be between the council

 For more information about NHS Continuing Healthcare in England, Wales and Scotland, see pages 182–4.

(as the funder) and the care home and your relative will have a copy of the terms and conditions of his or her stay. Ask the council for a copy of their contract with the care home to ensure it includes any special requirements that were noted in the care plan produced following your relative's assessment.

With the NHS

If your relative has been assessed as needing NHS Continuing Healthcare (see pages 182–4), the NHS is responsible for meeting the full cost of the care in a care home, or other setting. The Primary Care Trust (PCT) in the area in which your relative's GP practice is located is responsible for arranging and paying for your relative's care and accommodation. They will have a contract with the care home to pay the full fees.

❝ All care homes are regulated and each must provide prescribed information about the home in a suitable language and format. ❞

NATIONAL MINIMUM STANDARDS

All care homes in England, Wales, Scotland and Northern Ireland are now regulated in accordance with their own national standards and each care home must provide prescribed information about the home. This includes a contract or terms and conditions that is made available in a language and format suitable for the prospective resident. There is a slight variation in the standards for each country.

WHAT THE CONTRACT INCLUDES

Regardless of who is paying the fees, the contract should include:

- The room your relative will occupy.
- The terms and conditions of occupancy (short term, long term, intermediate care, respite care), including the period of notice.
- The care and services (including food and laundry) covered by the fee.
- How the care home will meet your relative's special requirements, such as dietary or religious needs.
- The fees or charges payable, how often and when the fees are due.
- Who pays the fees – your relative, the local council, the health authority, a relative or other third party.

To see the 'National minimum standards for care homes for older people' (England), go to www.csci.org.uk; for Wales, go to www.csiw.wales.gov.uk; for 'National care standards for Scotland', go to www.carecommission.com; and for Northern Ireland go to www.rqia.org.uk/publications/useful_documents.cfm.

Negotiating a fair contract

Increase in fees

Care homes are required to notify residents of any increase in fees and the reason for the increase. They have to give at least one month's advance notice or, if this is not practical because the timing of the increase is outside the care home's control, as much notice as possible. Examples of when the increase is outside the care home's control include where there is an imposed change to the funding arrangements or where the service has to change quickly to meet a resident's needs.

- Any additional services (including toiletries and equipment) to be paid for over and above those included in the fees.
- The rights and obligations of your relative and the care home and who is liable if there is a breach of contract.
- How your relative's money and valuables will be secured and who is responsible for insuring them.
- How changes to your relative's care needs will be managed.
- Whether there will be a charge for holding your relative's bed if he or she is away from the home temporarily.
- What happens if something goes wrong; how would you or your relative make a complaint?

UNFAIR TERMS

These are terms that may appear in a standard contract, about which your relative has no choice and which give the care home too much advantage over your relative. Unfair terms are often hidden in the detail of the contract. For example, they may:

- Seek to exclude the care home's legal liabilities.
- Impose unfair penalties, restrictions or obligations on your relative.
- Be unclear about what your relative has to pay.

Potentially unfair terms in a care home contract

The following terms may be potentially unfair. If any of them are in the contract your relative is asked to sign, they should be challenged if the care home:

- Is excluded from liability for causing death or injury.
- Excludes itself from providing a service.
- Is excluded from looking after your relative's property and possessions.
- If the care home excludes itself from responsibility if your relative's clothes are damaged in the laundry.
- Is allowed to make significant changes to what it supplies to your relative without consultation.

 To find your local Trading Standards Office, go to www.tradingstandards.gov.uk, and to find your local CAB, go to www.citizensadvice.org.uk.

Good contract policy

Here are some specific terms that should appear in a clear, transparent contract.

Notice periods

- Notice periods should generally be the same for your relative as for the care home.
- The grounds on which notice can be given as well as arrangements for refunding fees should be clearly stated.
- If there is a change in your relative's needs, which the care home cannot meet, the contract should be clear about whether your relative or the care home should give notice.
- Acceptable reasons for termination of the contract would include:
  - Voluntary decision by your relative.
  - The need for your relative to move to accommodation that can better meet his or her needs.
  - The need for your relative to go into hospital or other care at short notice.
  - Death of your relative.
  - Breach of contract for not paying the fees.
- If the home terminates the contract for reasons other than a serious breach by your relative, it is required to inform his or her next of kin and to give enough notice for your relative to find alternative accommodation.
- The process of giving notice should be clear and should allow for shorter notice periods in extreme cases.
- Where a prospective resident cancels an agreement and is in breach of contract, the care home is legally required to take reasonable steps to reduce its loss and the resident should not be required to pay more in compensation for defaulting on a contract than is needed to cover the loss caused to the care home.

Guarantors/sponsors

- Any contract requiring a sponsor to sign a guarantee should clearly state:
  - Who is liable to pay the fees.
  - In what circumstances these fees are payable.
  - The situations in which the guarantor has liability under the agreement.

Reservation fee or retainer

- Where a reservation fee or retainer is required, for example, if your relative is in hospital, the contract should state clearly what the care home will provide for it.

Payment of fees on death

- The contract should state the period for which fees remain due after the death of a resident or after his or her room is cleared. As this can vary from one home to another, it may influence the choice of a home.
- Fees are often paid monthly in advance and therefore the policy on refunds in the event of death should be clearly stated.

- Can change your relative's room without consultation.
- Can impose unreasonable restrictions or obligations on your relative.
- Has the right to keep or dispose of your relative's property or possessions.

In addition, you should challenge the terms if:

- Staff can enter your relative's room without their consent.
- It is not made clear how much your relative will have to pay, how often he or she will have to pay and who is responsible for payment.
- The terms are not clear about how long the fees are payable after death.

If you are unhappy with any aspect of the contract your relative is being asked to sign, uncertain about a specific term or need advice about challenging the contract, contact your local Trading Standards Office, CAB or social care registration authority (see page 151).

The Office of Fair Trading (OFT) has a duty to consider all complaints sent to them about unfair terms in consumer contracts. Since 1999, enforcement has been shared with other bodies, including UK statutory regulatory bodies, the trading standards service and Which?. If the OFT considers a contract term to be unfair, they have the power to take action on behalf of consumers in general to stop its continued use; if necessary by seeking a court injunction (or an interdict in Scotland). The OFT cannot seek redress for individuals. In 2005, over 800 care homes undertook to change standard terms in their contracts following OFT guidance on unfair terms in care home contracts.

❝ If you are unhappy with any aspect of the contract, talk to your local Trading Standards Office, CAB or social care registration authority. ❞

 For OFT guidance on unfair terms in care home contracts (2003) and 'Fair terms for care – a guide to unfair terms in privately funded care home contracts' (OFT 2004), go to www.oft.gov.uk.

Making a complaint

If you or your relative have a complaint, it is important that you talk to the most appropriate organisation.

IN A CARE HOME

Most people who live in a care home receive the care and support they need. However, things can go wrong. If your relative is unhappy with anything, it is always a good idea for him or her to talk to the person most involved. This gives the opportunity to address the problem at an early stage. If, for whatever reason, this is not possible or not successful, all care homes registered in England, Wales, Scotland or Northern Ireland are required to have a complaints procedure.

The complaints procedure

Homes must ensure that all residents have a copy of the procedure and know who to talk to and how to make a complaint. All complaints procedures should contain an assurance that no resident will be penalised in any way because of complaining. However, residents and their representatives can still be very reticent to make a complaint because they fear it will affect the quality of their care or that they will be victimised. As complaining can jeopardise relationships, it is important to be clear what you or your relative want to achieve through a complaint.

Step 1 If possible, encourage your relative, perhaps with your support, to talk to his or her key worker or a senior member of staff at the home or use the residents' committee or a 'suggestions box' (if there is one).

Step 2 If that initial discussion does not resolve the problem, raise the issue with the manager of the home, making sure he or she has your relative's concerns in writing together with all the necessary information. If possible, ask for a

---

Does your relative have grounds for a complaint?

If your relative is complaining, you may want to satisfy yourself that he or she has the grounds for a complaint. Take your relative somewhere private, such as to his or her room, and ask about what happened in as much detail as is possible, including who was involved and where the event happened. You will then have your own way of gently probing to check whether there are indeed grounds for making a complaint.

response within ten working days and keep a copy of the letter. Be clear what your relative is complaining about. If the home does not sort out the problem informally, you or your relative may want to make a formal complaint to the home.

Step 3 If you are unhappy with the care home's response, you can contact the social care registration authority, which can decide what action is necessary and can work with the care home to ensure they meet their legal obligations where complaints are concerned. The social care registration authority can also use its powers of inspection to undertake further enquiries.

If the local council is contributing towards your relative's care home fees, you can raise your concerns with them as well as the care home and the registration authority. In this case, you also have the option of using the local council's complaints procedure (see opposite).

Case Study Mrs Harris's mother

Mrs Harris's mother was 91, living in a care home in the Midlands and the highlight of her day was going into the dining room for her lunch. Unfortunately, she fell and broke her hip and spent some time in hospital. When she returned to the care home she needed a lot more help because she was mentally and physically frail. The staff arranged for her to have her lunch in the upstairs lounge where she sat for most of the day, and where staff were available to help her.

Mrs Harris was concerned to see that all the residents in the upstairs lounge had their lunch on trays fitted over their armchairs. She asked the staff if they could take her mother into the dining room, but they said she needed too much help. So Mrs Harris talked to the manager about her concerns that the frail residents did not move from their armchairs to a proper table for their lunch.

When that was not successful, Mrs Harris made a formal complaint under the care home's complaints procedure. The manager responded that there was not enough room to provide a proper table. Mrs Harris was unhappy and so contacted the Commission for Social Care Inspection (CSCI) (see page 151) and explained her concerns. CSCI inspectors made an unannounced visit to the home shortly afterwards and their subsequent report noted that action was required in relation to the upstairs lounge and several other environmental issues.

Several months later the manager left and the new manager started a programme of consultation with residents and relatives based on the inspection report. This led to quite a few improvements to the home, including a proper dining room for the more frail residents.

AGAINST THE LOCAL COUNCIL

Each local council should produce a leaflet explaining how to make a complaint, what to expect and setting timescales for each step of the process. This leaflet should be available at all council offices. Each council's procedure will differ slightly but there are usually three stages to the local council's complaints procedure.

Step 1 The informal stage. Contact the care manager or person concerned with your relative's care to see if the problem can be sorted out satisfactorily. Ask for his or her response to be put in writing.

Step 2 If you are not happy with the response, register your complaint formally. Your relative can do this or ask someone to complain on his or her behalf. The complaint will be dealt with by a service head or director. The service head should contact you or your relative within 28 days either with a response to your complaint or with an explanation as to why there is a delay.

In some cases, the council may want to arrange a meeting with you or your relative. If this is the case, take someone else along with you, perhaps another relative, friend or representative from an local advice agency such as Age Concern, to take some notes.

Complaints procedures outside England

In Wales, these are substantially the same as in England: stage 1 is dealt with at the local office, stage 2 is a formal complaint and is reviewed by an independent person unconnected with the council, stage 3 is an independent panel meeting, which can be convened if the complaint has not been resolved within three months. The local council is obliged to take account of the findings of the independent review but not to act on them. For more information, see the Social Services Complaints Procedure (Wales) Regulations 2005 at www.opsi.gov.uk/legislation/wales/wsi2005/20053366e.htm.

In Scotland, these are also substantially the same as in England but the three stages are called: informal resolution, local resolution and independent review. In Scotland there is no automatic right to an independent review – the complaints officer will advise you and your relative. The website www.spso.org.uk includes a complaint agency finder to ensure your complaint is directed to the correct agency.

In Northern Ireland, all Health and Social Services Trusts have nominated complaints officers. The three stages are informal discussion with the staff dealing with your relative and then their manager, local resolution and then an independent review. More information is on www.nhssb.n-i.nhs.uk/board/complaints.php.

Step 3 If you are not satisfied with the outcome of your formal complaint, ask for your complaint to be taken to a review panel meeting. You and/or your relative will be asked to attend the panel meeting and should always take someone with you as an independent witness. The review panel should record its conclusion within 24 hours of the meeting or ask for a formal extension. The panel recommendation will be reported to the director of adult services, who will then make a decision based on the panel's recommendation.

THE NHS COMPLAINTS PROCEDURE

Complaints about services or treatments from the NHS using the NHS complaints procedure must be made within certain time limits:

- Within six months of the event you are complaining about, or

---

Taking it further

The monitoring officer: All councils have a monitoring officer whose duty is to investigate any decision made within the council that may be illegal. The monitoring officer is usually a senior member of staff in the council's legal department and if you think a council decision is illegal, you can ask the monitoring officer to investigate. You may want to contact an independent advice agency before taking this route.

Local government ombudsman: The local government ombudsman can look into complaints about failures in the administrative systems and processes of the local council. There are strict rules about the type of complaint that an ombudsman can investigate and the ombudsman will not usually investigate your complaint unless it has been through the council's complaints procedure first. To find out more about the role of the local government ombudsman and how to further a complaint, go to www.lgo.org.uk. In Wales, it is the Public Service Ombudsman for Wales (www.ombudsman-wales.org.uk); in Scotland, the Scottish Public Service Ombudsman (www.spso.org.uk); in Northern Ireland, the Northern Ireland Ombudsman (www.ni-ombudsman.org.uk).

Local councillor: You or your relative can also get in touch with your local concillor. The civic centre or library will have contact details.

 For more information on making complaints via PALS, go to www.pals.nhs.uk, click on the link to 'About PALS' and then again on 'Resolving concerns'. You can also find your local PALS office on this website.

- Within six months of finding out about the right to complain, providing it is within 12 months of the event.

Lack of care in hospital or at discharge

If you are unhappy about your relative's hospital care or how his or her discharge was dealt with, you can use the NHS complaints procedure – the hospital can provide information about the process or go to the website for the Department of Health: www.dh.gov.uk.

The local Patient Advice and Liaison Services (PALS) office (see below opposite) can also help resolve issues at an early stage and can advise on the complaints procedure. If you want to make a complaint to the NHS that includes issues relating to the local council, the NHS can, with your permission, transfer any relevant part of the complaint to the local council. You should be told which part of your complaint the council will handle.

Challenging the decision not to grant your relative NHS Continuing Healthcare

If your relative has been refused NHS Continuing Healthcare funding, you should ask to see the assessment, the completed decision support tool and the criteria on which the decision was based.

If you are not able to get copies of these documents, contact your relative's local PALS. If once you have seen these documents you are still unhappy with the decision, write to the chief executive of your relative's PCT and ask for the case to be reviewed by the PCT review panel, stating clearly that you consider your relative has primary health needs that fit the criteria for NHS Continuing Healthcare.

If you still wish to challenge the decision, you can ask for your relative's case to be heard by the Strategic Health Authority's Independent Review Panel. PALS (see opposite bottom) can give you help and advice with the process.

If you still disagree, you can take your complaint to the Health Service Ombudsman. The Health Service Ombudsman will not investigate any complaints until they have been through the NHS complaints procedure.

IF YOU SUSPECT OR WITNESS ABUSE

One of the most difficult areas in which you, as a relative, may need to make a complaint is if you suspect or witness abuse of your relative or another resident.

Abuse is a single or repeated act or lack of appropriate action that is done to an older person, usually committed by

In Scotland, CABs are now funded by local NHS Boards to deliver the Independent Advice and Support Service (IASS). IASS aims to support patients, carers and relatives in their dealing with the NHS and other matters affecting their health. To find out more, go to www.cas.org.uk.

someone who is in a position of control or authority over the older person, such as a relative, carer or member of staff in a care home. An older person in a care home is particularly vulnerable.

Abuse of an older person can take several forms:

- **Physical abuse,** which may include hitting or rough handling, but can also include giving too much medication to make the older person drowsy and easier to look after or using furniture to stop them moving.
- **Financial abuse** includes illegal or improper use of an older person's property or valuables.
- **Sexual abuse** includes forcing an older person into sexual activity he or she does not want, including looking at books or videos.
- **Psychological abuse** includes intimidation by shouting, frightening or ignoring them, swearing, ridiculing them or blaming the older person for actions or behaviour he or she is not able to control.

It is abusive to deprive someone of food, clothes, warmth, hygiene needs or leave someone unattended for periods of time if that puts him or her at risk or causes distress or anxiety.

An older person is likely to feel frightened and intimidated as a result of being abused. He or she may not be able to seek help or tell anyone what is happening. Your relative may also need someone to take action on his or her behalf.

If you witness abuse

If you are visiting a care home and see abuse, challenge the person abusing the resident immediately and ask him or her to stop, write down what you saw, what you said, the dates and times and any other relevant details. Ask for a private meeting with the manager or other senior staff you can trust and explain what you saw. If you are not satisfied, ask for copy of the home's complaints procedure and use it. In severe cases, contact the social care registration authority and/or the local council.

If you suspect abuse of your relative

If your relative has told you about things that upset or frightened him or her:

- **Talk to your relative somewhere private,** such as a bedroom or possibly the garden.
- **Get as much detail** from your relative as possible (probing gently if necessary) about what is upsetting him or her, what happened, who was involved.
- **Suggest you both talk to his or her key worker**/nominated staff member or a member of staff that your relative trusts.

Ask for an explanation or an investigation. If you are not satisfied with the result, go to the relevant social care registration authority – the Commission for Social Care Inspection (CSCI) (England), the Care Commission (Scotland), the Care Standards Inspectorate for Wales or the

The Relatives and Residents Association (R&RA)

Relatives often need a listening ear to cope with feelings of guilt about their perceived inability to carry on caring. They may want to know how to get help in understanding the complex rules and regulations about paying for care or to complain about the quality of care that their loved ones are receiving. If this is you, the Relatives and Residents Association (R&RA) is a charity that might be able to give support and advice.

Go to www.relres.org for more information or ring the advice line: 020 7359 8136.

Regulation and Quality Improvement Authority (Northern Ireland) – immediately (see below). Do not wait for their next inspection and follow their advice.

If abuse is taking place or if you are not satisfied that action is being taken, you can also contact the local council. All councils in England and Wales have procedures for dealing with abuse of vulnerable adults under the local Protection of Vulnerable Adults Scheme (POVA). In Scotland, the Adult Support and Protection Act 2007 and the Protection of Vulnerable Groups Act 2007 give local councils and adult protection committees the authority to intervene where they consider a vulnerable adult is at risk or experiencing abuse.

If you need to meet with inspectors, local council staff or care home managers, follow the list of suggestions given to the right.

- Make sure a friend, relative or other person you trust is present.
- Seek an independent advocate. Contact Older People's Advocacy Alliance for details of local advocacy services at www.opaal.org.uk.
- At the meeting outline your cause (or causes) for concern.
- Ask what action will be taken.
- Ask how your relative will be protected while an investigation takes place.
- State you would like to be kept informed about the progress of the investigation and ask for this information in writing.
- Make your own written notes of what was said, including dates and times and who said what (or ask the person accompanying you to do so).
- Ask for an interpreter to be present if English is not your first language.

For more information about the social care registration authorities visit www.csci.org.uk (England); www.cssiw.org.uk (Wales); www.carecommission.com (Scotland); www.rqia.org.uk (Northern Ireland). See also page 151.

Glossary

Abbeyfield: A charity that runs housing with support for older people.

Almshouses: Charitable trusts that offer low cost accommodation aimed at older people.

Arms Length Management Organisations (ALMOs): Companies set up and owned by local councils to manage and improve their housing stock.

Assessed income period: The period after which your relative's entitlement to pension credit is reviewed, normally five years.

Assessed needs: Those care needs that fall within the local council's eligibility criteria.

Capital threshold: The amount of capital your relative is allowed to have before it affects his or her entitlements.

Care manager: The person, usually employed by the local council, responsible for assessing your relative's needs and ensuring he or she receives the services agreed in the care plan. Sometimes called a social worker.

Care package: The mixture of care and support services, often from different agencies, such as social services, the housing department and NHS, that your relative receives.

Care plan: A written summary of your relative's assessed needs, setting out what support he or she should receive, when, why and who should provide it.

Contribution record: The National Insurance contributions (NIC) paid.

Court of Protection: A court that makes decisions relating to the property and affairs as well as healthcare and personal welfare of people who lack capacity. It also has the power to make declarations about whether someone has the capacity to make a particular decision.

Direct payments: The money given by local councils to people who have been assessed as needing community care services. Direct payments enable people to buy and manage their own services.

Disabled facilities grant (DFG): A means-tested grant given by councils to enable the homes of disabled homeowners and private tenants to be adapted to meet their needs.

Discretionary trust: Where money or assets are held in trust and payments from the trust are made wholly at the discretion of the trustees and there is no absolute entitlement either to capital or income.

Dissolved: Closed down.

Domiciliary care: Services provided in your relative's own home. They are also called community care services or home care services.

Drawdown: A facility to take money from an equity release scheme as needed, rather than in a lump sum.

Duty social work team: The staff team that takes requests for social services help when there is no member of staff actively working with a particular older person.

Eligibility criteria: The local council's rules describing who qualifies for services provided or arranged by them. Eligibility criteria are set by councillors and may vary each financial year.

Extra care housing: Self-contained accommodation for older people with personal care, meals and 24 hour support available for those that need it. Also called very sheltered housing.

Financial assessment: See means test.

Ground rent: Sum payable annually by the leaseholder to the landlord in addition to the service charge.

Industrial and provident societies: Organisations conducting a trade or business and registered by the Financial Services Authority under the Industrial and Provident Societies Act 1965.

Joint tenancy: Joint tenants jointly own the whole property and on death of one of the joint owners, his or her interest in it automatically passes to the other as if it were in trust for them. Most properties bought by married couples are held as joint tenancies.

Lasting Power of Attorney: A legal document stating that a third party is able to control someone else's affairs (their finance, care and welfare).

Lease: The legal contract between the freeholder (landlord) and leaseholder, giving the leaseholder the right to live in the flat for a specific number of years.

Leasehold: The purchase of a lease.

Means test: The council's method of determining the amount your relative should pay towards the cost of his or her care services. The council asks for information about your relative's income and savings and then works out how much he or she should pay towards the services. Also called a financial assessment or charging procedure.

Mixed tenure: Retirement housing that has some properties to buy (leasehold), some to rent and some identified for shared ownership. They are mainly owned by housing associations.

Needs assessment: The process by which the local council or NHS gathers together and records all the relevant information about the help and support your relative may need.

NHS Continuing Healthcare: A care package of services provided and paid for by the NHS for people who have very complex health needs.

Office of the Public Guardian (OPG): A public service that helps protect people who lack mental capacity by setting up, managing and monitoring the actions of Lasting and Enduring Powers of Attorney and appointing deputies.

Ordinarily resident: A phrase that means 'where your relative usually lives'. This is the council that is usually responsible for assessing your relative's needs and paying for any care.

Primary Care Trust (PCT): A part of the NHS that is responsible for health services, such as GPs, dentists, opticians, mental health services, pharmacies and primary and community health services.

Qualifying year: A tax year in which sufficient national insurance contributions (NIC) have been paid or credited to qualify for it to be counted towards a State Pension.

Reduced basic pension: Paid to those who have not paid sufficient NIC to qualify for a full State Pension, but have paid at least a quarter of the qualifying years needed.

Respite care: A service provided to an older person to enable his or her carer to have a break from the caring responsibilities.

Retirement housing: Self-contained accommodation for older people that usually includes support, such as an alarm system and scheme manager. Retirement housing is also known as sheltered housing, warden-assisted or warden-controlled housing.

Scheme manager: The person employed to manage a retirement housing scheme.

Self-funder: Someone who is paying his or her own care fees, such as in a care home.

Shared ownership: An arrangement that allows your relative to buy a proportion of his or her home and rent the rest from the landlord. Usually only available through housing associations. Also known as part ownership or part rent/part buy.

Sheltered housing: See retirement housing.

Social care: The support given or arranged for people who need help to live as independently and normally as possible, to maintain their health and wellbeing and to take part in family and community life.

Social Fund: A government scheme to help people with needs they cannot meet out of regular income.

Social housing: Housing provided by local councils and housing associations.

Social services department: A department of the local council that is responsible for assessing needs for community care services; arranging or providing these services and providing financial support to older and disabled people following a financial assessment. The department is sometimes called Adult Services.

Tariff income: Income that is derived from capital.

Tenants in common: Joint ownership of property where each joint tenant owns a separate share in the property, typically 50:50, and consequently they can will their separate share to whoever they wish.

Third-party top up: The amount that is needed to pay the difference between the local council's standard rate for a care home and the actual care home fees. Also called a third-party contribution.

Trust Corporation: A legal body that provides professional legal services.

Warden: See scheme manager.
Wound up: Discontinued.

Useful addresses

Abbeyfield Society
Abbeyfield House
53 Victoria St
St Albans
Herts AL1 3UW
Tel: 01727 857536
www.abbeyfield.com

Advice Information and Mediation Service (AIMS)
Tel: 0845 600 2001.
www.ageconcern.org.uk/aims.asp
See also *Age Concern England* (below)

Age Concern
England
Astral House
1268 London Road
Norbury
London SW16 4ER
Tel: 020 8679 8000
Information line: 0800 00 99 66
www.ageconcern.org.uk

Northern Ireland
3 Lower Crescent
Belfast BT7 1NR
Tel: 028 90 24 57 29
www.ageconcernni.org

Scotland
Causewayside House
160 Causewayside
Edinburgh EH9 1PR
Scottish Helpline for older people: 0845
125 9732
Textphone: 0845 2265851
www.ageconcernscotland.org.uk

Wales
Ty John Pathy
13–14 Neptune Court
Vanguard Way
Cardiff CF24 5PJ
Tel: 029 2043 1555
www.accymru.org.uk

Association of Retirement Housing Managers (ARHM)
Southbank House
Black Prince Road
London SE1 7SJ
Tel: 020 7463 0660
www.arhm.org

Care and Repair Scotland
135 Buchanan Street
Suite 2.5
Glasgow G1 2JA
Tel: 0141 221 9879
www.careandrepairscotland.co.uk

Citizens Advice (CAB)
Look in your local telephone book or go to:
www.adviceguide.org.uk (England and Wales)
www.citizensadvice.co.uk (Northern Ireland)
www.cas.org.uk (Scotland)

Counsel and Care
Twyman House
16 Bonny Street
London NW1 9PG
Advice line: 0845 300 7585
www.counselandcare.org.uk

Department of Health
Richmond House
79 Whitehall
London SW1A 2NS
Customer Services: 020 7210 4850
www.dh.gov.uk

Department for Work and Pensions (DWP)
Enquiry Line: 0800 88 22 00
www.dwp.gov.uk

Directgov
www.direct.gov.uk

Disabled Living Foundation
380–384 Harrow Road
London W9 2HU
Helpline: 0845 130 9177
www.dlf.org.uk

Elderly Accommodation Counsel (EAC)
3rd Floor
89 Albert Embankment
London SE1 7TP
Advice line: 020 7820 1343
www.HousingCare.org

Financial Services Authority (FSA)
25 The North Colonnade
Canary Wharf
London E14 5HS
Consumer helpline: 0845 606 123
www.fsa.gov.uk
To find a local IFA, go to: www.unbiased.co.uk

First Stop Care Advice
Advice line: 0800 377 70 70
www.firststopcareadvice.org.uk

Foundations
Bleaklow House
Howard Town Mill
Glossop
Derbyshire SK13 8HT
Tel: 01457 891909
www.foundations.uk.com

Help the Aged
England
207–221 Pentonville Road
London N1 9UZ
Tel: 020 7278 1114
Advice line: 0808 800 6565
www.helptheaged.org.uk

Northern Ireland
Ascot House, Shaftesbury Square
Belfast BT2 7DB
Tel: 02890 230 666
Advice line): 0808 808 7575

Scotland
11 Granton Square
Edinburgh EH5 1HX
Tel: 0131 551 6331

Wales
12 Cathedral Rd
Cardiff CF11 9LJ
Tel: 02920 346 550

Care Fees Advice
Care advice line: 0500 76 74 76
www.helptheaged.org.uk/carefees

Housing Corporation
149 Tottenham Court Road
London W1T 7BN
Tel: 0845 230 7000
www.housingcorp.gov.uk

Leasehold Advisory Service (LEASE)
31 Worship Street
London EC2A 2DX
Tel: 020 7374 5380
www.lease-advice.org

National Association of Estate Agents
(NAEA)
Arbon House, 6 Tournament Court
Edgehill Drive
Warwick CV34 6LG
Tel: 01926 496800
www.naea.co.uk

National Centre for Independent Living (NCIL)
4th Floor, Hampton House
20 Albert Embankment
London SE1 7TJ
Tel: 0207 587 1663
www.ncil.org.uk

National Health Service
www.nhs.uk
www.wales.nhs.uk (Wales)
www.show.scot.nhs.uk (Scotland)
www.hscni.net (Northern Ireland)

NHFA Care Fees Advice
Care advice line: 0800 99 88 33
www.nhfa.co.uk

Northern Ireland Housing Executive
Belfast Area Office
32–36 Great Victoria Street
Belfast BT2 7BA
Tel: 08448920900
www.nihe.gov.uk

Office of Fair Trading (OFT)
Fleetbank House
2–6 Salisbury Square
London EC4Y 8JX
Tel: 08457 22 44 99
www.oft.gov.uk

Office of the Public Guardian (OPG)
Archway Tower
2 Junction Road
London N19 5SZ
Tel: 0845 330 2900
www.publicguardian.gov.uk

Ombudsman services
Housing Ombudsman Service (HOS) England
81 Aldwych
London WC2B 4HN
Tel: 0845 7125973
www.ihos.org.uk

Local Government Ombudsman (England)
PO Box 4771
Coventry CV4 OEH
Tel: 0845 602 1983
www.lgo.org.uk

Northern Ireland Ombudsman
The Ombudsman
Freepost BEL 1478
Belfast BT1 6BR
Tel: 0800 34 34 24 (freephone)
www.ni-ombudsman.org.uk

Public Service Ombudsman for Wales
1 Ffordd yr Hen Gae
Pencoed CF35 5LJ
Tel: 01656 641 150
www.ombudsman-wales.org.uk

Scottish Public Services Ombudsman
SPSO
Freepost EH641
Edinburgh EH3 OBR
Tel: 0800 377 7330
www.spso.org.uk

Pension Service (England, Wales and Scotland)
Tel: 0845 60 60 265
Benefits enquiry line: 0800 882 200
Benefits enquiry line (Northern Ireland): 0800 220 674
www.thepensionservice.gov.uk
Pension tracing service: 0845 600 2537
In Northern Ireland, contact the Department for Social Development: www.dsdni.gov.uk

Relatives and Residents Association (R&RA)
24 The Ivories
6–18 Northampton Street
London N1 2HY
Advice line: 020 7359 8136
www.relres.org

Royal National Institute for Deaf People (RNID)
19–23 Featherstone Street
London EC1Y 8SL
Freephone: 0808 808 0123
www.rnid.org.uk

Royal National Institute of Blind People (RNIB)
105 Judd Street
London WC1H 9NE
Helpline tel: 0845 766 9999
www.rnib.org.uk

Safe Home Income Plans (SHIP)
83 Victoria Street,
London SW1H 0HW
Tel: 0870 241 60 60
www.ship-ltd.org

Scottish Executive
Housing Division
2 Victoria Quay
Edinburgh EH6 6QQ
General enquiries tel: 08457 741 741
www.scotland.gov.uk

Shelter
Housing advice helpline: 0808 800 4444 (England and Scotland), 0845 075 5005 (Wales), 028 9024 5640 (Northern Ireland)
http://england.shelter.org.uk
http://northernireland.shelter.org.uk
http://scotland.shelter.org.uk
www.sheltercymru.org.uk

Social care registration authorities
Care and Social Services Inspectorate Wales
Cathays Park
Cardiff CF10 3NQ
Tel: 01443 848450
www.cssiw.org.uk

Commission for Social Care Inspection (CSCI) (England)
33 Greycoat Street
London SW1P 2QF
Tel: 020 7979 2000
Helpline: 0845 015 0120
www.csci.org.uk (England)

Regulation and Quality Improvement Authority (Northern Ireland)
9th floor Riverside Tower
5 Lanyon Place
Belfast BT1 3BT
Tel: 028 9051 7500
www.rqia.org.uk

Scottish Commission for the Regulation of Care
The Care Commission
Compass House
11 Riverside Drive
Dundee DD1 4NY
Tel: 0845 603 0890
www.carecommission.com

United Kingdom Homecare Association (UKHCA)
Group House
2nd floor
52 Sutton Court Road
Sutton
Surrey SM1 4SL
Helpline: 020 8288 5291
www.ukhca.co.uk

Welsh Assembly Government
http://new.wales.gov.uk

Index

which?

Which? is the leading independent consumer champion in the UK.
A not-for-profit organisation, we exist to make individuals as powerful as the
organisations they deal with in everyday life. The next few pages give you a
taster of our many products and services. For more information, log onto
www.which.co.uk or call 0800 252 100.

Which? Online

www.which.co.uk gives you access to all Which? content online and much, much more.
It's updated regularly, so you can read hundreds of product reports and Best Buy
recommendations, keep up to date with Which? campaigns, compare products, use our
financial planning tools and search for the best cars on the market. You can also access
reviews from *The Good Food Guide*, register for email updates and browse our online
shop – so what are you waiting for? To subscribe, go to www.which.co.uk.

Which? Legal Service

Which? Legal Service offers immediate access to first-class legal advice at unrivalled
value. One low-cost annual subscription allows members to enjoy unlimited legal advice
by telephone on a wide variety of legal topics, including consumer law – problems with
goods and services, employment law, holiday problems, neighbour disputes, parking,
speeding and clamping fines and tenancy advice for private residential tenants in England
and Wales. To subscribe, call the membership hotline: 0800 252 100 or go to
www.whichlegalservice.co.uk.

Which? Money

Whether you want to boost your pension, make your savings work harder or simply need
to find the best credit card, *Which? Money* has the information you need. *Which? Money*
offers you honest, unbiased reviews of the best (and worst) new personal finance deals,
from bank accounts to loans, credit cards to savings accounts. Throughout the magazine
you will find tips and ideas to make your budget go further plus dozens of Best Buys. To
subscribe, go to www.whichmoney.magazine.co.uk.

which?

Which? Books

Other books in this series

NEW EDITION Buy, Sell and Move House
Kate Faulkner
ISBN: 978 1 84490 056 5
Price £10.99

This new edition of the Which? best-selling property guide covers the latest changes to HIPs and analysis of the property market. From dealing with estate agents to chasing solicitors and working out the true cost of your move, this guide tells you how to keep things on track and avoid painful sticking points.

What to Do When Someone Dies
Paul Harris
ISBN: 978 1 84490 028 2
Price £10.99

Coping with bereavement is never easy but this book makes dealing with the formalities as straightforward and simple as possible. Covering all the practicalities, *What to Do When Someone Dies* provides step-by-step guidance on registering a death, making funeral arrangements, applying for probate and sorting out financial matters.

Wills and Probate
Paul Elmhirst
ISBN: 978 1 84490 033 6
Price £10.99

Wills and Probate provides clear, easy-to-follow guidance on the main provisions to make in a will and the factors you should consider when drafting these. You will also find advice on probate, making the process as straightforward and trouble free as possible. By being aware of key changes and avoiding the common problems and pitfalls, you can limit delays, avoid disputes and save tax.

which?

Which? Books

Other books in this series

Giving and Inheriting
Jonquil Lowe
ISBN: 978 1 84490 032 9
Price £10.99

Inheritance tax (IHT) is becoming a major worry for more and more people. *Giving and Inheriting* is an essential guide to estate planning and tax liability, offering up-to-the-minute advice from an acknowledged financial expert. This book also features information on equity release, trusts and lifetime gifts.

NEW EDITION Renting and Letting
Kate Faulkner
ISBN: 978 1 84490 054 1
Price £10.99

A practical guide for landlords, tenants and anybody considering the buy-to-let market. Written by an experienced property professional, this real-world guide covers all the legal and financial matters, including tax, record-keeping and mortgages, as well as disputes and security. This new edition features the latest on energy performance certificates and tenancy deposit protection schemes.

Tax Handbook 2008/9
Tony Levene
ISBN: 978 1 84490 045 9
Price £10.99

Make sense of the complicated rules, legislation and red tape with *Tax Handbook 2008/9*. Written by the *Guardian* personal finance journalist and award-winning consumer champion Tony Levene, this guide gives expert advice on all aspects of the UK tax system and does the legwork for you. It includes information on finding the right accountant and how to get the best from them, NI contributions, tax credits for families and the self-assessment form. This new edition also contains updates from the 2008 budget and guidance on how green taxes could affect you.

Which? Books

Which? Books provide impartial, expert advice on everyday
matters from finance to law, property to major life events.
We also publish the country's most trusted restaurant
guide, *The Good Food Guide*. To find out more about Which?
Books, log on to www.which.co.uk or call 01903 828557.

**"Which? tackles the issues that really matter
to consumers and gives you the advice and active
support you need to buy the right products."**